INSIDE, OUTSIDE, AND ONLINE

Building Your Library Community

Chrystie Hill

FOREWORD BY *Steven Cohen*

American Library Association

CHICAGO 2009

Chrystie Hill is a librarian, writer, and community builder. After a short stint at the Seattle Public Library, she started It Girl Consulting, a small venture that helps libraries use online tools to build communities online. In 2003 Chrystie joined WebJunction, where she serves as director of community services. Chrystie is a frequent presenter at library meetings and conferences, and her articles have appeared in *JASIST* (*Journal of the American Society for Information Science and Technology*), Library Journal, and RUSQ (Research and User Services Quarterly). In 2007, Chrystie was nominated a Library Journal Mover and Shaker. Chrystie holds an MA from Sarah Lawrence College, and her MLIS is from the University of Washington, Seattle, where she lives with her desk and a laptop. You can follow her blog at http://librariesbuildcommunities.org.

The paper used in this publication meets the minimum requirements of American National Standard for Information Sciences—Permanence of Paper for Printed Library Materials, ANSI Z39.48-1992. ∞

Library of Congress Cataloging-in-Publication Data
    Inside, outside, and online : building your library community / Chrystie Hill ; foreword by Steven Cohen.
       p. cm.
    Includes bibliographical references and index.
    ISBN 978-0-8389-0987-4 (alk. paper)
    1. Libraries and community—United States. 2. Libraries and community—United States—Case studies. I. Title.
Z716.4.H55 2009
021.2—dc22   2008052520

ISBN-13: 978-0-8389-0987-4

Printed in the United States of America
13 12 11 10 09   5 4 3 2 1

This work is dedicated to the colleagues whose thoughtful considerations were pivotal to my moving forward through some part of it. I am very fortunate to be a part of changing libraries and our profession with you.

Also, for Rose.

CONTENTS

FOREWORD

LIBRARIES BUILD COMMUNITIES. The phrase has always made my spine tingle with joy whenever I read the words or hear it uttered by colleagues. Three very powerful words indeed.

When I first became a page in a public library at the ripe age of sixteen, I thought that the library was about books. To be sure, this was the reason I joined the profession. But when I started sitting behind the reference desk, answering random questions from the public and assisting with community-based projects, I knew that the library was about much more than just books.

I have since left public libraries behind, but they still play an integral part in my life. As many Saturdays as possible, I bring my daughter and son to our local library. We read books, play games on the computers, put together puzzles, and enjoy random chitchat with the librarians (many of whom know me from my professional activities). When I am there alone, picking up books for my commute, I am always thrilled to see such a vibrant community involved in library activities, whether it be seniors exercising, mommy and me classes, or book discussion groups. The library is the center, and it does indeed build a community.

I first approached Chrystie with the idea of writing a community-building book after several lengthy, and sometimes loud, discussions about various library topics. I knew that she was involved in community-building practices after reading her beautifully written article on the topic in *Library Journal* (www.libraryjournal.com/article/CA502019.html). I had been thinking about approaching ALA with a book about social networking (online and off) and public libraries, but I had a feeling in my gut that it needed something more. After reading Chrystie's article, I knew what the book needed: an expert to write it with me, and someone who could bring in the community-centered approach. I have since moved on from my research and writing on community building (I changed jobs and my focus is now on helping build a small but growing law library management business), and my time was precious with a growing family, so I bowed out of the project. Chrystie continued on the venture, and I am thrilled to see it come to fruition.

This book is mainly about storytelling around community building and how librarians from all over the world have succeeded in making the library the center of their circle. Interviews were conducted with both those who were sought out and those who approached the author—stories that fulfill a theme that has been slowly penetrating our communities. Social capital theories based on the need to communicate with one another face to face and not "bowl alone" brought a need for public and academic libraries around the world to fill the void. And, based on what we read in this book, the need is being satisfied.

Community building is essential to any library, be it public, academic, or special, especially during a time when many don't see libraries' value. Beyond just marketing their services, libraries that build community will thrive and continue to be relevant for a very long time. And this book can be the guiding light.

Steven Cohen
December 2008

PREFACE

Libraries Build Communities—A Personal Perspective

Books and materials are really secondary in a library. The most important aspect is the human interaction. The library experience cannot be viewed as just an information transaction, but rather as an opportunity to touch and connect lives.
—Cheryl Napsha, Director, William P. Faust Public Library, Westland, Michigan

I BECAME INTERESTED IN LIBRARIES and community building while working toward my MLIS at the University of Washington's newly minted iSchool. I remember the look of puzzled bewilderment from Joe Janes, with whom I had worked as a graduate research assistant. During one of our last conversations, he asked, "What do you want to do next?" "Libraries are good, but I want them to matter," I remember saying. "I want them to connect communities and support democracy." I know why he was puzzled. We had spent the last twenty-four months feverishly researching digital reference services, both on library websites and elsewhere on the Web, and I had shown interest in and promise as a "digital librarian." It's true that I was at least as interested if not more engaged in technology and the changes that digitization had brought to traditional library services. I'm not sure Joe expected me to regurgitate what some would say were worn-out clichés about democracy, change, and public libraries.

My adherence to perhaps simplistic but still noble professional ambitions for myself and for libraries was influenced in part by the Bill and Melinda Gates Foundation's investment in public access computing and libraries, which I had witnessed since 1997. Hailing from the Seattle area and having a large number of friends and acquaintances working as field trainers for the U.S. Libraries Program, I became intimately familiar with the challenges inherent in providing library service (especially public access computing) to small, rural towns and the people who live in them. While setting up networks and training library staff across the country, I learned through observation and conversation with my colleagues that staff members in small, rural libraries struggled to provide adequate access to information (including digital) as well as to create a common place or "community center" for the people they served. In many cases they were also struggling to articulate the value of their libraries to their communities; just as libraries were being called on by Gates to offer access to the Internet, the Internet became the reason they were called on by their communities to close. Staff at small and rural libraries had been asked to address a dramatic shift in their roles within the community. Previously dependent on an outdated set of encyclopedias, perhaps missing volume M, to answer reference questions, they were suddenly providing access to the world's information, and it was globally and immediately both accessible and distributable. The needs were immeasurable, as were the challenges in meeting them. Still, I understood and held in high regard the critical service that library staff in small and rural libraries had taken on with new grace and acumen. To me these people were nothing short of public heroes, working through technology to practice the tenets of our profession to provide access to knowledge and information in support of democratic ideals. So while I had been thoroughly engaged in learning how emerging technologies were changing our profession and our services, my real love was for public libraries.

Unfortunately, my first foray into public service challenged me to maintain these ideals, not just for library service in small and rural areas but for library service in general. I first worked for a large library system's central branch with more than two dozen intercity branches, and in spite of the strong leadership and vision of the city librarian, I frequently found myself entangled in run-ins with middle managers and supporting staff. One colleague, responding to my glee at having answered a reference question with a Google search, expressed the sentiment (not kidding) that "every computer in every public library should be bludgeoned with a sledgehammer." On reviewing my annual work plan, which included establishing "standard reference practices for all patron requests" for our department, my supervisor said, quite simply, "You're too ambitious." (Two years later, the library formed a committee to do just that.) It wasn't long before I realized that the environment, combined with my role there, would support neither my interest in technology innovation nor better quality public services. To be fair, some of my colleagues in the same system found the ability to do more.

I promptly found gainful employment in a private sector company, developing a web-based information product with an online community component. The company was looking for someone with professional research skills and passion for "the relationship between theory, practice, and organization change." Sounded like me; they agreed. Our mission was to assist organizations with change, learning, and partnerships in the context of an online peer-based community of practice. Inspired by Peter Senge and Etienne Wegner, I supported our mission and was enchanted by the possibility of working with a group that wouldn't mind if I were "too ambitious." All was well until we realized that we weren't going to make it through the dot-com bust. The last employee standing, I handed over my single disk of digital files capturing the years of work we had done together, set up shop as an independent consultant, and hit the job and client search scene. Within a year a former colleague from my time in public libraries referred me to a friend of hers who had just received a Bill and Melinda Gates Foundation grant to "develop an online community for library staff." I was intrigued. Fifteen minutes later I was on the phone with the project content manager; a week later I was hired as the second Seattle-based staff member for the project now known as WebJunction.org.

Since its inception and over the course of my time there, WebJunction has grown to include (at the time of this writing) dozens of library agency partners, more than 40,000 library staff members, and nearly 70,000 unique visitors per month. Initially our focus was on creating an online community for library staff who were recipients of the original Gates Foundation grants, particularly those working in small and rural libraries to support public access computing. Over time the project has grown to include library staff members from fifteen countries and from every type of library, covering and contributing content and resources on everything from library policy and management to patron services to practical, emerging technologies for libraries. During the course of my work at WebJunction, I reconnected to my interest in technology and its impact on library services, as well as to the notion that the library is a critical stakeholder in the communities we serve. As librarians and as community builders, we facilitate important relationships between people and content, as well as between individuals; we do this with technology, with community partnerships, and physically within library spaces. I firmly believe that although the tools and the tactics we use to create these connections have changed, our essential role within the communities we serve has not.

In 2004, while attending the first OCLC-sponsored Blog Salon at an ALA annual conference, I met Steven Cohen, a prolific writer and author of the blog *Library Stuff* (www.librarystuff.net). Steven had noticed my declaration earlier that same year that participating in professional online communities took us back "to the roots of our profession" (Hill 2005). He'd blogged after reading it that he "stood up and clapped," and so I was anxious to meet such a prominent player in the biblioblogosphere who had also recognized my work. Without delay, Steven and I entered a spirited disagreement about the prevalence and relevance of electronic library lists and the communities there. "Library lists are dead!" announced Cohen, much to my dismay. "PUBLIB has 6,000 subscribers!" I countered, citing examples of connection and relevance there. Later I asked Cohen to review another article that I'd written for *Library Journal* about libraries, community building, and our perhaps misplaced love and adoration of technology tools used to accomplish our objectives. Instead of providing feedback on the article, Steven picked up the phone: "Do you want to write a book?" he asked. "Yes," I replied. We talked to our editors at ALA Editions, and this project began.

As we progressed through the project, Steven increasingly moved on to pursue personal and family priorities. I am grateful to him for originating the concept with me, articulating the project's questions and approach, conducting early research, and writing the foreword to the work. Most important, I am grateful to the hundreds of library staff members I came to know during the course of this project. Their work and their willingness to share it are ensuring that all libraries can change, matter, and thrive.

The book begins by setting our research in context with broader scholarship, research, and trends. I look at networks, technology, and community and at some of the ways both people and libraries are impacted by recent developments in these areas. In the next chapter, I walk through the questions and implications recent issues have raised for library practice and the urgent need for libraries to consider their work through the lens and practice of building community. I briefly outline our research methods and the essential components of community building revealed by the library practitioners we worked with throughout the project. In chapters 3 through 7, I look at each component in more detail, again setting historical and scholarly context for the experiences relayed by our respondents.

My ambitions with this work are to continue the professional discourse on libraries and community building and to provoke further discussion about the librarian's essential role as purveyor of both *content* and *connection* for the communities we serve. I also hope to encourage our profession to actively share with and learn from one another so that libraries and our services stay relevant and sustainable through whatever change is ahead.

ACKNOWLEDGMENTS

My FIRST THANKS GO to the scholars and writers who inspire me. I'd like to thank Robert Putnam, who got me started on this topic with his exclusion of libraries in *Bowling Alone*. John Seely Brown, Ray Oldenburg, and Kathleen de la Peña McCook all contributed substantially to my continued interest in libraries and community building. Marylaine Block renewed my faith in this project with *The Thriving Library*. Thanks also to the Bill and Melinda Gates Foundation and to OCLC for their ongoing commitment to libraries, and without whom this work would not be possible.

Thanks to Steven Cohen for arguing with me at the first Blog Salon about whether or not "library lists are dead!" He made this work possible by suggesting we start it together. When it came time for him to step out of the project, he did so with grace and aplomb. I appreciate his thoughtfulness in the foreword and final work.

Thanks to Roy Tennant, Rachel Singer Gordon, Rebecca Miller, Walt Crawford, Jenni Fry, and especially Patrick Hogan for shepherding me through my first contract and publication. Thanks to Brian Bannon, Kathleen de la Peña McCook, Rachel Van Noord, Michael Porter, Helene Blowers, Marilyn Mason, Sharon Streams, Jennifer Peterson, Meredith Farkas, and Chris Jowaisas for talking me through various sections or conceptual obstacles. J. Michael Jeffers and Carolyn Crabtree brought it all home.

Thanks to the hundreds of librarians and library staff who contributed to "Libraries Build Communities." Your sharing made it possible to uncover the essentials of community building in libraries. My colleagues at WebJunction (all past and present) inspired me with their good humor, teamwork, and commitment; I've learned more about community building from you than from anyone. Sarah Reynolds and my e-group helped me articulate for the first time that I wanted to write a book and supported me through much of the process. Thanks to Brian Bannon and Zac Ray for creating space for my writing retreats in their home.

My work would not be possible without the support of my friends and family, with special thanks to Mom, Dad, Rose and Heather, Andrew, and Trudee.

I would not be possible without the delightful, considerate, and loyal Aaron J. Briggs.

CHAPTER ONE

People and Networks

At present the tendency is to conceive individual mind as a function of social life. . . . [Reading, writing, and arithmetic] are social in a double sense. They represent the tools which society has evolved in the past as the instruments of its intellectual pursuits. They represent the keys which will unlock to the child the wealth of social capital which lies beyond the possible range of his limited individual experience.
—John Dewey, "The Psychology of Elementary Education,"
in *The School and Society,* 1900

It's easy to take the offline communities to your online communities. If the library's challenge is to acquire new patrons, you'll find them in cyberspace. Go and get the patrons where they are.
—Britta Biedermann, Head Librarian, Sociology Library,
University of Zurich

PUBLIC DISCOURSE AROUND SOCIAL ACTIVITY, networking, community building, and public service has grown over the last decade, calling into question the roles of libraries and librarians in society and in relation to the communities we serve. From my perspective, three major factors are contributing to this discourse. First is the popularization of social science research, reflected in such books as Robert Putnam's *Bowling Alone* and Ray Oldenburg's *The Great Good Place.* Second is the Gates Foundation's investment in libraries and public access computing, and third is the popularity of participatory media and social networking on the Web. At first glance these factors may seem disjointed, but they come together to form a particular crossroads in both the perception and actualization of contemporary library services. Together, they evoke essential questions about what the library does, how we should be doing it, where we should be doing it, and for whom.

1

Since the publication of Robert Putnam's *Bowling Alone* (2000), there has been a growing perception that, at least for Americans, community and civic engagement is in decline. In his book, Putnam describes how, over the past thirty years, Americans have increasingly stopped voting, joining political parties and service organizations, and attending community meetings. Commuting, increasing work demands, and technology, Putnam argues, all have a role in the decline. In short, we join bowling leagues less; we watch television more. Putnam's and other's works raised public awareness about the meanings and uses of *social capital,* its relationship to building social networks, and the core qualities of strong communities. Library professionals responded to these works, most often lamenting that the library had not been exposed as an exemplary builder of social capital for its neighbors.

During the same period, libraries were, perhaps understandably, somewhat distracted, and this may explain why we were a part but not in the center of community-building discussions. We were grappling with what may prove to be the most critical change impacting library service in the past century: the emergence of computing as "standard fare" service in libraries (Stevenson 2007). According to recent research on public libraries and the Internet, nearly "100 percent of public library outlets in the U.S. are connected to the Internet" compared to only 44.6 percent in 1997 (Bertot et al. 2007). More than 14 million people regularly use public library computers to access the Internet to meet personal information needs; computer use trends in special and academic libraries are not as thoroughly understood.

The Bill and Melinda Gates Foundation is largely responsible for the prevalence of public access computing in public libraries. Beginning in 1997 with the goal of "ensuring that if you can get to a public library, you can access the Internet to learn, explore opportunities, and enrich your life," phase I of the foundation's program placed more than 11,000 computers in 40,000 public libraries across the United States and Canada by the time of the program's completion in 2003. Phase II of the program initiated another five-year grant period, beginning in 2007. In this next step, the foundation hopes to "help public libraries stay connected" and "maintain high-quality computer and Internet access." However, the grantors also claim that these will be "the last grants given by the foundation to fund computer upgrades in U.S. public libraries with vulnerable technology" (Gates Foundation 2008).

But what were library patrons and other information consumers *doing* with all that Internet access? With all those networks? Briefly, they were searching for, and finding, *themselves,* many of them doing so for the first time in libraries. And this leads us to the third factor converging with "social capital" and "computing as library service" discourse. Within this same time frame, the Internet has essentially "come of age" in the United States and beyond (De Rosa et al. 2007). Research indicates that, worldwide, more and more of us spend at least some time on the Internet connecting with others, searching, purchasing, and even creating or publishing our own digital content.

Since the publication of Putnam's *Bowling Alone*, the Internet and web-based technologies have all but completely penetrated interactions with commerce, discovery, and even personal relationships. The increasing prevalence of e-mail, electronic lists, blogs, wikis, social networking, and social media on the Web has moved us away from an environment in which Internet access merely encourages users to find themselves. Instead, it's provoking us to find ourselves. By facilitating collaboration and communication with other users, the social Web is pushing everyone, not just libraries, to determine and articulate their place in a new media world. This chapter looks at each of these trends as a backdrop to our research and conversations with library staff actively building community through libraries.

SOCIAL CAPITAL: WHAT IT IS AND WHY IT MATTERS TO LIBRARIES

"Developing the 'I' into 'We'"

The term *social capital* is relatively new to popular discourse and is still not easily defined. It has been referred to as the adhesive, glue, bind, or grease of human relationships and the value derived from those connections. Although references to the term can be traced to Marx, more recent contributions come from academic sociologists.[1] In 1986, Pierre Bourdieu identified three distinct forms of capital: economic, cultural, and social. He saw social capital as a "durable network" characteristic of the elite and that generally functioned as "a mask" for profit seeking and became a means by which the powerful remained so (Bourdieu 1986). A few years later James Coleman (1988) elaborated on Bourdieu's concept by discerning the potential value of connections for all people, regardless of their status as privileged or disadvantaged. While Bourdieu had a somewhat sinister view of the privileged using their social capital to retain the status quo, Coleman acknowledged that disadvantaged groups could benefit from their connections and relationships as well. Coleman presented the possibility that some institutions or structures might be better suited to the creation of social capital in that they were more apt to cultivate reciprocity, trust, and individual actions within the network. Both Bourdieu and Coleman brought discussions of social capital into academic discourse, making way for new conceptualizations, definitions, and qualitative explorations.

Political and social scientist Robert Putnam is responsible for popularizing the term *social capital* a decade later. Beginning with *Making Democracy Work: Civic Traditions in Modern Italy* (1993), Putnam and his colleagues explored contemporary government institutions in Italy and argued that the "horizontal bonds" that make up social capital are critical to the quality of civic life and the cultivation of a democratic society. Putnam then turned his explorations to civic life in the United States and published "Bowling Alone: America's Declining Social Capital" in the *Journal of Democracy*. In his article, Putnam conceptualizes social capital—as advanced through a "rapidly growing body of work"—as the "features of social organization such as networks, norms, and social trust that facilitate coordination and cooperation for mutual benefit" (1995, 67). Putnam claims that in networks with social capital, individual lives are easier and everyday business transactions are less costly.

> For a variety of reasons, life is easier in a community blessed with a substantial stock of social capital. In the first place, networks of civic engagement foster sturdy norms of generalized reciprocity and encourage the emergence of social trust. Such networks facilitate coordination and communication, amplify reputations, and thus allow dilemmas of collective action to be resolved. When economic and political negotiation is embedded in dense networks of social interaction, incentives for opportunism are reduced. At the same time, networks of civic engagement embody past success at collaboration, which can serve as a cultural template for future collaboration. Finally, dense networks of interaction probably broaden the participants' sense of self, developing the "I" into the "we," or (in the language of rational-choice theorists) enhancing the participants' "taste" for collective benefits. (67)

In 2000, Putnam published a book-length expansion of the original article: *Bowling Alone: The Collapse and Revival of American Community*. In this work he further explains social capital as the collective benefit derived from participation in social networks. "Like any other form of capital," Putnam argues, social capital allows for productivity of individuals and groups in civil society. And it has as its "conceptual cousin, 'community.'" Putnam further explains that "social capital greases the wheels that allow communities to advance smoothly. Where people are trusting and trustworthy, and where they are subject to repeated interactions with fellow citizens, everyday business and social transactions are less costly" (288). In his 2004 history of the term, James Farr boils down Putnam's social capital as comprising networks, norms, and social trust. Over time, summarizes Farr, "networks prove dense and valuable, . . . norms pervade individual actions and social relations, and trust appears" (8).

In *Bowling Alone* Putnam expands his argument that social capital had substantially declined in America since the late 1960s. He argues that Americans have become disconnected from family, friends, neighbors, associations, and democratic structures, evidenced in that people were eating dinner together and having guests less often, that they had stopped signing petitions or joining clubs and leagues. But why? Putnam argues that people work too much, move too often, and spend more time with TV and the Internet, leaving less time for *interactions with other people*. Putnam raises concerns about communities continuing to support one another and effectively resolve conflicts without social capital. "Americans," he writes, "need to reconnect with one another" (28). In conclusion Putnam offers a few suggestions for reversing these trends.

Putnam's use and expansion of the concept of social capital received wide attention, initiating policy and research discussions about social capital among popular audiences for the first time. Referred to as "pathbreaking," "controversial," and "alarmist" at once, "Bowling Alone" is generally regarded as "the most widely discussed social science journal article of our time" (Wolfe 1999). The follow-on work elicited passionate and critical responses from social and political scientists as well as the popular press. Putnam appeared simultaneously in *People* magazine and President Clinton's White House, even receiving an invitation to Camp David. Responses to Putnam's work were described by Alan Wolfe in the *New York Times* as "quasi-religious in nature" (1999). Since their publication, both works have garnered thousands of citations and elicited as many critical responses and an ongoing debate about the meanings and use of the term *social capital* as well as its purported decline.[2]

More recently, John Field simplified the notion of social capital. "The theory of social capital," he writes, "at heart, is most straightforward. Its central thesis can be summed up in two words: 'relationships matter'" (2003, 1).

By making connections with one another and keeping these connections going over time, people are able to work together to achieve things that they either could not achieve by themselves or could achieve only with great difficulty. People connect through a series of networks, and they tend to share common values with other members of these networks; to the extent that these networks constitute a resource, they can be seen as forming a kind of capital. As well as being useful in its immediate context, this stock of capital can often be drawn on in other settings. In general, the more people you know and the more you share a common outlook with them, the richer you are in social capital.

Around the same time Putnam was doing his research, American sociologist Ray Oldenburg was working on *The Great Good Place*. In this work, Oldenburg explores the bars, coffee shops, main streets, corner stores, and other "third places" that host and facilitate "regular, voluntary, informal, and happily anticipated gatherings . . . beyond the realms of home and work" (1989, 16). Articulating his own version of "relationships matter," Oldenburg claims that third places promote social equality by leveling status, provide a setting for public conversation, create habits of association, and offer psychological support to individuals and communities. "The character of a third place is determined most of all by its regular clientele and is marked by a playful mood, which contrasts with people's more serious involvement in other spheres. Though a radically different kind of setting for a home, the third place is remarkably similar to a good home in the psychological comfort and support that it extends" (42). Third places, Oldenburg argues, are the heart of a community's social vitality.

Library professionals and scholars joined this conversation, immediately noting specifically that libraries had been left out. Drawing on this awareness and on widespread sentiments after the September 11 attacks in New York City, Nancy Kranich, in the November 2001 issue of *Library Journal*, pointed out "a unique, if fleeting, opportunity to carve out a *new* mission as creators of social capital." She wrote, "Americans have a renewed need to connect and rebuild trust," and "librarians have the place and the resources to enable connection." Hoping to incite our profession to clear, deliberate action toward "civic awareness and community revival," Kranich argued that libraries could be the key social institutions or "commons" where citizens could speak freely, share concerns, or pursue their individual and community interests. "The challenge is to gain the skills necessary to be effective, active facilitators and collaborators. After they build the networks and the trust, librarians will have to assess our ongoing impact and that of the institution on solving community problems" (41). Most important, she concluded, we must demonstrate and articulate how we make a difference.

In *American Libraries* that same fall, Jean Preer pointedly asked, "Where are libraries in *Bowling Alone*?" and advocated that libraries take a more visible and active role in creating what Putnam had identified as both bridging and bonding social capital (Preer 2001). Library users, she pointed out, are active in their communities, and communities with strong libraries rank high on social capital indicators. "Libraries must be part of society's thinking about how we develop and nurture social as well as information networks," she concluded, while lamenting that libraries are "simultaneously ignored and taken for granted" as both indicators and creators of social capital. But these lamentations were not new, nor was this version of the purpose and place of the library, especially public libraries. Preer noted the concern of 1934 ALA president Gratia A. Countryman that libraries had escaped the attention of the author of *Recent Social Trends*, a mammoth study of American life published the previous year. "'What have we done or not done that this can be so?'" Countryman asked. "'Why is it that we have not impressed ourselves, as an important and essential institution, upon the governing body or upon intelligent authors and scholars? Is it in the very nature of our work that it should be so, or is it in ourselves?'" (Preer 2001, 62).

Three-quarters of a century later, Sarah Long designated "Libraries Build Communities" as her ALA presidential theme for the year 2000, and Kathleen de la Peña McCook published *A Place at the Table: Participating in Community Building* (2000), in which she challenged librarians to make up for the dismissal of other community building theorists, activists, and planners by "get[ting] involved early and often by demanding a place at the community planning and development table." A year later, Ronald McCabe argued for *civic librarianship* in which the traditional mission of the public library is to serve as a pivotal social institution, community center, and essential component of civil society (McCabe 2001). Without directly examining the reasons for the lack of awareness of the library's ongoing role in civic engagement, Preer and other library scholars placed us in the conversation and called for revisiting and reframing library missions, establishing our role in civic engagement, and furthering our advocacy efforts so that people would know what we were up to. Years later, the connection between the social networks and relationships that scholars, researchers, and practitioners identify as critical to building strong communities remains to be universally accepted by librarians *and* communities as a central tenet of our professional role.

THE LIBRARY LANDSCAPE

"Automating nineteenth-century librarianship"

I received my MLIS degree the same year Robert Putnam published *Bowling Alone.* Although librarians had been left out of his original work, we could all see the importance of his argument to our work and to our changing profession. But there's more to the story than a few professional responses to his work, even including the call to reframe or restore the library's social mission. The past two decades have also marked a massive and essential change for library services everywhere. With the Bill and Melinda Gates Foundation's investment and philanthropy in libraries through its U.S. Libraries program, nearly 50,000 computers were placed in almost 11,000 libraries between 1998 and 2003. But the Gates Foundation's philanthropy did more than put computers and Internet access in libraries. The program also trained approximately 60,000 library staff workers, provided live technical support, published materials and newsletters designed to support public access computing in libraries, and delivered more than $250 million in Microsoft software to libraries (although not without controversy; see Stevenson 2007).

Largely because of the Gates Foundation's philanthropy, public access computing was cinched as a core library service, and, by the end of the program, digital resources had become as essential to the library's collection as printed materials once were. According to research from Florida State University's Information Use Management and Policy Institute and its "Public Libraries and the Internet" study, although many libraries in the United States had embraced the importance of Internet access since the early 1990s, in 1994 only 21 percent of public libraries had an Internet connection. A decade later, Internet connectivity had jumped to 99.6 percent (and 98 percent of these libraries offered public access to their Internet services). Over the same period, the information infrastructure in libraries continued to develop as well, most markedly with the number of public workstations and the speed of Internet access provided. In 1998, only 3 percent of public libraries had ten or more graphical workstations. By 2007, the average number for all libraries was 10.7 (a figure that seems to indicate a plateau, as it has not changed significantly since 2002). Between 1998 and 2006, the number of public libraries offering Internet speeds of 56 Kbps or less had shifted from 65.6 percent to 2.1 percent. Researchers concluded that "as public demand and network-based applications resource requirements increased, public libraries kept pace with increased service and access" (Bertot et al. 2006). More recent data on Internet access in public libraries show that 99.7 percent of public library facilities are connected; 99.1 percent offer public access. Wireless public access is also on the rise, up from 36.7 percent in 2006 to 54.2 percent a year later. The "Public Libraries and the Internet" research also indicates that public libraries planned to add, replace, and upgrade workstations, as well as add wireless access in 2008 (Bertot et al. 2006, 2007).

At the risk of making an understatement, the Internet has changed library services considerably, but not in the ways I may have liked. As the Internet enabled what some have called a revolution in global distribution of and access to information, responsibilities for the organization and management of resources returned to the content creators (or owners). Our profession, in many ways, seemed impervious. Distracted, perhaps, by the nuts and bolts of getting and keeping public access computing up and running, meeting increasing demands for IT (information technology) service, and garnering further financial support for the sustainability of these programs, library staff seemed more concerned with fixing their printers and arguing about why users didn't find us as relevant as Google than they were with imagining the incredible opportunity before us: to lead and facilitate the content creation and discourse of our communities and constituents. "The library community," said one industry pundit, "is mostly in denial about real issues and questions" (De Rosa, Dempsey, and Wilson 2004, 9). In a 2003 report to its membership titled *Environmental Scan: Pattern Recognition*, OCLC further established that libraries were operating in a swiftly shifting information landscape and that we were somewhat disoriented by it. Scanning, the report proposed, would help us "discern patterns in the environment that will help us determine where we are and where we should go" (De Rosa, Dempsey, and Wilson 2004, x). The scan revealed three important social trends, indicating the prevalent values of contemporary information consumers: self-sufficiency, satisfaction, and seamlessness. First, people were more readily doing things for themselves online. Whereas individuals previously were dependent on librarians or other information professionals for both organization and access, they became empowered to devise their own delivery and reference services without the help of a professional mediator. Second, information consumers were typically satisfied with the information they were retrieving online. They found it more convenient, expedient, and good enough to meet most needs. Finally, the scan identified the convergence of work, home, and social life in the proliferation of interactive, always on, collaborative, and dynamic communication and content generation applications on the Web.

Meanwhile, the library had become increasingly difficult to characterize. We struggled to consistently describe the main purpose of the library, but worse, we failed to focus on the experiences of those using the library. "This too shall pass," said one library service agency director. "The constant questioning of a library's reason for existing is a very good thing. Libraries have continued to evolve to find their appropriate function—their core service" (De Rosa, Dempsey, and Wilson 2004, ix). Still, what had not changed was a strict belief that our traditional roles of organizing, rationalizing, and providing access to information were still necessary and good. That, and we were still holding on tight—primarily as the keepers and holders of content that's rare, difficult to distribute, or difficult to access. "Scarcity of information is the basis for the modern library," note the authors of the OCLC scan, but "contrast this world with the anarchy of the Web. The Web is free-associating, unrestricted and disorderly. . . . The two worlds," they conclude, "appear to be incompatible" (De Rosa, Dempsey, and Wilson 2004, ix). Indeed. Organization and control (through materials management) had characterized the library for as long as we could remember. The Web, on the other hand, was disorganized, disassociated, and dispersed.

Some libraries started to shift their focus away from the acquisition and ownership of the information they were responsible for. The most resilient of our profession responded by helping to organize decentralized resources on the Web (such as the Librarians' Internet Index at http://lii.org) and by helping to create better environments for Internet users to interact with other types of resources and professionals (such as the emergence of the Information Commons in college and university libraries). But we were far from removed from a collection-centric model, held fast to our preferred formats, and still struggled to provide context or other kinds of value to library users.

THE AGE OF PARTICIPATION

"You control the Information Age"

By this time (we're still in 2003), it may have already been too late. That year, the Pew Internet and American Life Project established that more than 60 percent of U.S. adults were already "going online to access the Internet or World Wide Web," and nearly three-quarters of those were considered "veterans" (those who had *three years' experience* on the Web). Between March 2000 and August 2003, the number of American adults going online increased by 47 percent, from 86 million to 126 million. On-line activities consistently grew over this period as well, with Internet users discovering "more things to do online as they gain[ed] experience and as new applications [became] available" (Madden 2003, i). That momentum produced further reliance on the Internet *in everyday life* as well as higher expectations about what the Internet should deliver and how it could be used.

Across the board, information-seeking activities increased by 50 per-cent between 2000 and 2003. Some users were seeking health or spiritual information, others looked for news, financial information, sports, or poli-tics. Others were banking online, looking for government information, or shopping. Still others were instant messaging or downloading multimedia. More than any other online activity, however, they were using e-mail, and many reported that "email use increase[d] their communication with key family and friends and enhance[d] their connection to them" (Madden 2003, ii). In 2003, nine in ten Americans had sent or read e-mail. Five in ten had tried instant messaging (IM), and nearly three in ten had tried chat rooms or online discussions. Yet, while the number of e-mail users trumped any other form of online communication, the growth of both chat room use and IM was nearly the same as that for e-mail, particularly for youth and for experienced users, indicating that we were about to see growth in these areas as well. Finally, two in ten (or approximately 21 million Internet us-ers) had created content for the Internet, and most of them had high-speed Internet access, were young adults, and had experience online. The report concluded that increased use was in part caused by the growth and preva-lence of high-speed Internet access, increased experience as an Internet user, and the increased amount of online content and applications. Very simply, "there [were] more ways to pursue everything online," and people were getting better at it.

> The Internet has been irrevocably woven into everyday life for many Americans. While there once was a time when the Internet was interesting because it was dazzling, it is now a normalized part of daily life for about two thirds of the U.S. population. . . . All the trends set out here seem destined to continue, if not evolve, as the technology gets better, the applications become simpler, and the appliances that use the Internet become omnipresent, and

the technology fades into the background of people's lives—as powerful, ubiquitous, commonplace, and "invisible" as electricity. (Madden 2003, 78)

Over the next three years, the participatory Web exploded into what has now been popularized by the term *Web 2.0*. Web 2.0 is described by Wikipedia as "changing trends in the use of World Wide Web technology and web design that aim to enhance creativity, information sharing, and collaboration among users," further marked by "the development and evolution of web-based communities and hosted services, such as social-networking sites, video sharing sites, wikis, blogs, and folksonomies." With numerous definitions, many of them contested, the term generally "encapsulates the idea of the proliferation of interconnection and social interactions on the Web." Taking users beyond independent content access and information retrieval, which they had been doing for quite some time, Web 2.0 facilitates content creation, ownership, augmentation, and control, as well as a high degree of self-representation and social interaction.

Throughout this period (2003–2006), Pew and other researchers considered the continued growth of Internet use almost entirely in the context of human engagement, interaction, and communication. "Does the Internet affect social capital in terms of social contact, civic engagement, and a sense of community?" they asked. Early research showed that online interaction increased social capital, civic engagement, and a sense of community online. The Internet augmented the frequency of face-to-face and telephone contact, and supplemented participation in voluntary organizations or politics, suggesting that "as the Internet is incorporated into the routine practices of everyday life," it is "quietly fostering the changing composition of social capital" as well as becoming "more geographically dispersed" (Quan-Haase et al. 2002, 320). In 2006, a report from the Pew Internet and American Life Project proclaimed that "the Internet helps build social capital . . . supports social networks . . . and promotes 'networked individualism'" (Boase et al. 2006). The study examined how the Internet and e-mail aid users in maintaining their social networks. "Instead of disappearing," the researchers claimed, "people's communities are transforming" (i).

This and related research showed that online communication and, more generally, connectivity was taking place with the same set of friends and family contacted in person and by phone, supporting the position that the Internet was aiding rather than damaging social connections. Further, in contrast to Putnam's claims, the research showed that half of all Americans have at least fifteen close, core ties. In addition, Americans have an average of twenty-seven somewhat close, significant ties. Keeping in touch with the people in these social networks takes place in person and by phone, cell phone, e-mail, and IM. For users with cell phones and Internet access, contact with their ties increased substantially. E-mail was more important to those with large social networks and networks that were geographically dispersed. E-mail users were communicating more often than recent generations and possibly more often than any previous generation. One impact of these trends was that people were more often getting help for their challenges, large and small. People were using their social networks to seek information and advice, and when they used cell phones or e-mail to do so, they were finding a smoother path to the information they sought. They were benefiting if they had developed a large network of somewhat close yet significant ties. In addition to helping Americans make life decisions, the Internet had also aided in the expansion of our connections with people overall.

Looking specifically at Web 2.0 technologies, Pew and other researchers noted that an increasing number of users were going online to self-publish content that they had created. And although users had been going online since 2002 to publish their photos to sites like Kodak Gallery, new socially integrated sites like Flickr and Photobucket were far surpassing more traditional sites, with radical growth and user acceptance. These applications, blogger Ross Mayfield noted, "are made of people," but Pew and other researchers showed us that, more than that, they are made of young people. "And whether we call the current world 2.0 or 10.0, there's no question that the Internet of today will look positively *beta* to future generations" (Madden and Fox 2006, 6). Not surprising, then, that *Time* magazine proclaimed "you" as its Person of the Year in 2006 over the caption, "You control the Information Age. Welcome to your world."

And if that's not enough to frighten your average library and information professional, I don't know what is.

NOTES

1. Although Putnam attributed the first use of the term to L. H. Hanifan, a rural school superintendent and Progressive Era (1890–1920) education reformer who was concerned with "goodwill, fellowship, mutual sympathy and social intercourse" among people in a small rural community "whose logical center is the school" (Halpern 2005, 6). James Farr (2004) traces the origins of the term to the philosopher, psychologist, and education reformer John

Dewey, well known for his progressive education activism and contributions to American pragmatism during the same period. Dewey argued that "traditional" education was not relevant to an individual without concern for his or her relation to others, groups, or society at large; that the physical school should be social; that the methods of teaching should be social; that "communication alone can create a great community." Both Hanifan's and Dewey's writings on education reform strike me as very similar to the contemporary discourse around technology, change, and social reform in libraries. Farr's analysis extends the use of the term all the way to late nineteenth-century political theorists, from Bellamy to Sidgwick to Marx, all of whom addressed "capital from the social point of view." Farr then calls for new considerations of work, sympathy, and education to carry forward the discourse around "social capital."

2. "*Bowling Alone* won't make Putnam any less controversial, but it may come to be known as a path-breaking work of scholarship, one whose influence has a long reach into the 21st century" (John J. Miller, Amazon.com Reviews); "One of the strongest bits of data confirming Putnam's alarmism" (Wolfe 1999); "But 'Bowling Alone' could never have generated the passionate responses it did had it not spoken to something in the atmosphere" (Wolfe 1999); "After critiquing neo-Tocquevillean analysts ['best captured by Putnam'] for neglecting the role of changing political context in influencing associational activity and social capital, they argue for a top-down approach in which purposive government initiatives can have the positive effect of enhancing and creating social capital" (Edwards, Foley, and Diani 2001); "The reaction to [Putnam's] essay was . . . quasi-religious in nature" (Wolfe 1999); "What accounts for Robert Putnam's notoriety? What about him could simultaneously interest Bill Clinton and *People* magazine?" (Zengerle 1997).

CHAPTER TWO

Libraries and Communities

Libraries should be about the people they're for, not about the services we think they need.
—Barbara Fister, Academic Librarian, Gustavus Adolphus College, St. Peter, Minnesota

I have nothing negative to say about the library. It just can't compete with individuals using computers to get information.
—Survey Respondent, OCLC *Environmental Scan 2003*

WHERE IS THE LIBRARY?

"Almost two billion served"

"IT'S A STORY ABOUT COMMUNITY and collaboration on a scale never seen before," quipped the 2006 "Person of the Year" article in *Time* magazine. Indeed. Yet again, where is the library?

As the Internet became embedded in our everyday lives, many more people became accustomed to using search engines, to communicating via e-mail, to finding their own information, to purchasing their books and airline tickets online, and even to using blogs, IM, or social networking and media sites to connect. It may even be boring to point it out, it's so mainstream. But what they stopped doing is thinking of the library as one of their information resources online. OCLC notes that between 2005 and 2007, using a library website was the only online activity that *declined* among those familiar with and having access to the Internet.

In contrast, over the same period, physical use of libraries increased, though not as dramatically as Internet use in general. "Predicted demise due to Internet fails to materialize," touts a 2007 ALA news release; "new data on U.S. libraries shows almost two billion served." In its 2007 *State of America's Libraries* report, ALA showed that the number of visits to public libraries increased 61 percent between 1994 and 2004, while circulation increased 28 percent over the same period (ALA 2007a). "Far from hurting American libraries, the Internet has actually helped to spur more people to use their local libraries," said ALA President Loriene Roy. "Libraries still serve a unique function in providing those who seek knowledge and information with guidance from trained and educated professionals" (ALA 2007b). Overall, library users reported that the primary reason they go to a library "is to check out or read books," but 44 percent of library users under age 35 report going to the library to use computers. When asked what would compel them to visit the library more often, "free classes and programs for people my age" topped the list, followed by the library being open more hours. People under age 35 also supported library cafes, more computer and online resources, and Internet access.

As ALA reports on library visits and circulation, OCLC examined perceptions of libraries by the public (De Rosa 2005). To learn more about library use, about awareness and use of electronic resources, and about the "library" brand, OCLC created an online survey that reached people familiar with online resources and with access to the Internet. The survey drew responses from 3,348 people in six countries. In the area of library use, 96 percent of respondents reported that they had visited a public library (ever), while only 27 percent had visited a library website. Thirty-one percent claimed to use the library regularly (from daily to monthly), 24 percent used the library "several times a year," and 45 percent claimed to visit the library either "at least" or "not even" once a year. OCLC also asked if library use had changed in the preceding three to five years. Many users (44 percent) indicated that their library use had stayed about the same, 25 percent claimed that their library use had increased, and 31 percent claimed their library use had gone down. If visits to the physical library were increasing, this research seemed to indicate that it was likely not by people who already had Internet access at work or at home (De Rosa 2005).

Still, "borrowing print books" was the library service that most (55 percent) respondents reported using most frequently, with "researching

Rank order results of more than 3,000 responses to the question, *How frequently do you use the library for the following reasons?*

1. Borrow print books
2. Research specific reference books
3. Get assistance with research
4. Read/borrow best seller
5. Get copies of articles/journals
6. Use online databases
7. Use the computer/Internet
8. Do homework/study

Cathy De Rosa, *Perceptions of Libraries and Information Resources: A Report to the OCLC Membership, 2005*

specific reference books" following (see the accompanying text box for full ranking). Most interesting, the OCLC *Perceptions* report sought to uncover the public's relationship with the library "brand." Across all regions surveyed, respondents unequivocally associated libraries first with books, and, the researchers were quick to point out, "*there is no runner up.*" However, when asked about the main purpose of the library, most (53 percent) people reported the library's purpose as "information" and 33 percent reported the library's purpose as "books." Forty-one percent of respondents had positive associations with books, materials, and information as library services, and 30 percent of respondents had negative associations with books, materials, and information as library services, perhaps indicating a resigned neutrality more than anything.

Respondents were also asked to give advice to libraries with the open-ended question, If you could provide one piece of advice to your library, what would it be? With answers ranging from "keep up!" to "smile" and "advertise," respondents offered invaluable advice for making the library more attractive to them as individual users. My favorite: *stop making it feel like church* (De Rosa 2005).

As a library professional, I value traditional library services and am as interested as most of my colleagues in whether library visits and overall circulation have increased. Yet, increased circulation and visits to the library, even an increase in library program or classroom attendance (especially for children's programs), feels less of a feat against the fact that we're not doing a good job online or outside the library. We're absent (not entirely, but mostly) as active community builders even in our own spaces, but certainly outside the library. We've neglected to recognize our role as organizers and keepers of information access as primarily a *social* role. In fact, the scholars engaged in early discussions about the role of the library in developing and facilitating the participatory and social nature of the Web weren't librarians, and the year was 1996.

In their seminal work "The Social Life of Documents," John Seely Brown and Paul Duguid explained that documents—digital or otherwise—are much more than carriers of information. Although documents are powerful for helping us structure and organize information space, they also help us create and negotiate social space. In other words, groups form and conversations emerge around them. Brown and Duguid argued that we should expand our notion of the document to include all the social interaction that happens around it. Here they are in the late 1990s, well before Web 2.0 *or* prevalent Internet use, telling us that if we pay attention to how people form groups and create community around documents, it will help us move technology (and by extension, other services) in the direction of what humans actually do with a document (Brown and Duguid 1996, 2000). In my version of the story of *where we went wrong,* my first point is this: we've neglected to consider, in general, the social life of documents, as outlined in the article. This is true for all documents, regardless of format.

A few anecdotes from some target users are instructive:

Trudee is a young professional, presently in her early twenties. She won't ask a librarian any question, at any time, for any reason. *I can ask my friends or find it myself,* she says on the suggestion that she ask a reference librarian to help her solve a problem or locate information; *they're faster.*

Matt is a middle manager, presently in his early thirties, who also trained as a librarian. Upon discussing whether his local library is relevant to him, he says (quite emphatically), *the most important information need that I have is "what are my friends doing?"* concluding then that the public library is not relevant to him as an individual user.

In the words of one OCLC survey respondent, presently in her early forties: *Books, books, books, rows and rows of books, stacks of*

books, tables filled with books, people holding books, people checking
out books. Libraries are all about books. That is what I think and
that is what I will always think.

Somewhere along the way we chose (deliberately or otherwise) to
value our traditional roles as much as we valued the traditional definition of the documents we cared for. If documents helped humans structure and organize information space, librarians helped humans structure,
organize, and access documents. In neglecting the social nature of documents and our users, we neglected to nurture, or at least to articulate, the
very social nature of our own roles. A look at the ALA presidential themes
over the period drives home this point (see the text box "ALA Presidential
Themes, 1990–2008"). Although some themes point to empowerment,
community, service, and equity for people using libraries, more often the

---

ALA PRESIDENTIAL THEMES, 1990–2008

Kids Who Read Succeed
Your Right to Know: Librarians Make It Happen
Empowering People through Libraries
Customer Service: The Heart of the Library
Libraries: An American Value
Equity on the Information Superhighway
Kids Can't Wait for Library Service
Global Reach . . . Local Touch
Celebrating the Freedom to Read! Learn! Connect!
Libraries Build Community
Libraries: Cornerstone of Democracy
Gatekeepers of the Information Age: From Safety Net to
   Springboard
Save America's Libraries; Better Salaries and Pay Equity
Equity of Access
Stand Up and Speak Out for Libraries
Library Education and Diversity Recruitment
Libraries Transform Communities
Celebrating Community, Collaboration, and Culture

presidential themes focus on document access and materials delivery, greatly underestimating for our funders and our constituents the powerful position we are also in to facilitate, collaborate, and connect.

And all this leaves us squarely out of the loop.

WHAT IS A LIBRARY?

"Stuff, Place, Service, Interactions, Values"

For starters, I think we've been asking the wrong question. Instead of repeatedly asking, "Where is the library?" we should be asking, "*What* is a library?"

Recently, University of Washington iSchool professor Joe Janes spoke about what it means to be *in* the library. He posed the possibility that a library is defined as "stuff, place, service, interactions, and values." When materials and collections were not digital but were literally and physically stored on shelves and (at best) delivered through interlibrary loan, the place and the stuff were more critical to the definition, purpose, and brand of libraries. As materials and collections become ever more digitized, our collections and services become increasingly available outside the library, and sometimes at the drop of a hat. As a result, the place that was once the library also comes under scrutiny and, in the best-case scenario, starts to change. And it's here that our service, values, and the interactions we facilitate become even more important to our ongoing relevance.

At the time of this writing, the most recent research from the Pew Internet and American Life Project on Internet activity and adoption in the United States (through May 2008) shows that, since 1995, Internet use by American adults has steadily grown from around 15 percent to 73 percent (Pew Internet and American Life Project 2008). Internet World Stats, a website that regularly reports on population and Internet use, corroborates Pew's findings, reporting 72.5 percent of Americans using the Internet according to Nielsen's net ratings in June 2008. That's currently more than 220 million Americans "at least occasionally" online. For young adults ages 18 to 29, the figure increases substantially to 90 percent online. The more education you have, the more suburban your lifestyle, and the more income you have, the more likely you are to be online (Madden 2006).

OCLC researchers surveyed more than 6,000 members of the public in six countries about online activities and confirmed these figures: nearly 90 percent of their respondents had been online for four years or more, and a quarter had been online for ten years (De Rosa et al. 2007). OCLC's researchers also confirmed that e-mail (97 percent) and searching (90 percent) are mainstays of everyday life with the Internet, but they pointed out that the general population of Internet users is increasingly and actively communicating, interacting, and participating in content creation on the Web. Of those surveyed, 51 percent had used IM, 46 percent had blogged, 37 percent had used a social networking site (such as Facebook), and 32 percent had used a social media site (such as Flickr). Twenty percent of the total public had created a web page and indicated their main reason for doing so was "to communicate with friends and family."

> Technology must support the relationship and community-building efforts of the library, else there isn't much use for it.
>
> William C. Barrow, Special Collections Librarian, Cleveland State University, Ohio

If our distraction with computing in libraries explains why we're not at the table, it does—some would say paradoxically—allow us to put ourselves back into a central community-building role. In spite of the hubbub over the library's core mission being compromised or endangered by computing, particularly social computing, I argue that it takes us back to the core tenets of librarianship and connects us unequivocally to traditional library services that have been building community locally at least since the Progressive Era and the turn of the last century. Returning to Kranich's conclusion in *Libraries Create Social Capital,*

The challenge for librarians is to gain the skills necessary to be effective, active facilitators and collaborators. After they have built the networks and the trust, librarians will have to assess their ongoing impact and that of the institution solving community problems. They will have to immerse themselves in the civic life sprouting around them. They will have to initiate and expand partnerships that help connect citizens and bridge differences. Most important, librarians must demonstrate and articulate to officials and the public just how libraries make a difference. They need to prove how libraries contribute to the social capital required to engage citizens in the life of their communities. (2001, 41)

If computing explains why we're still not entirely at the table, let social computing be the reason to once again place ourselves irrevocably in the center of that discourse.

LIBRARIES BUILD COMMUNITIES: A SURVEY OF COMMUNITY BUILDING IN LIBRARIES TODAY

> Think outside the box! Don't get hemmed in by thinking things aren't "what libraries do." We don't just provide books or Internet services—we help the community. And we can do that in more ways than we're used to doing.
>
> Mary Doud, Deputy Director, Kalamazoo Public Library, Michigan

Steven Cohen and I came to this work with a set of questions that we believed were critical to the future of libraries and to the definition of the librarian's role in the twenty-first century: What is the library's role in building community and developing social networks? Has the library's role in community building changed over time? And how does this relate to our other role as content providers? Finally, how does technology, especially web-based technology, impact this role?

To answer these questions, we first turned to Robert Putnam and other writers defining social capital and its relation to community building and civic engagement. Next, we examined the library landscape and the shifting forces of technology and economic change, especially as they impact our roles in both content fulfillment and community building. Finally, and perhaps most important, we surveyed, interviewed, or visited hundreds of library staff members to learn about their community-building work in libraries. Over the course of this research, we uncovered five common practices among library practitioners actively pursuing their work through a community-building lens. In very simple terms, these common practices are to assess, deliver, engage, iterate, and sustain. We found that approaching library services with the intention of building community allows library practitioners to systematically evaluate and iterate library service to better meet individual and community needs. In short, our patrons and communities are better served and better connected, and so is the library.

Each concept is discussed briefly here, and each is further examined in subsequent chapters. And if you're looking for more practical applications, consider the following questions before moving through the rest of this work. They may jump-start your thinking about how some of these ideas and examples can come into play in your library.

Assess. Understanding user needs is key to community-focused library service. Needs assessment plays a significant role in matching library services to community needs. The next chapter will outline a basic process for both formal and informal needs assessment and discuss analysis of findings. Once your community needs are identified, you're ready to match them back to existing or new library services. Key questions to consider before diving into this section:

- When was the last time your library conducted a needs assessment?
- Did the needs assessment attempt to assess the needs of the entire community or a subset?
- What methods of assessment were used?
- What were the assessment findings and how were they analyzed?

Deliver. The next component involves strategically serving communities based on their needs. This component includes strategic planning, collection development, program and service development, and resource management. Considering our users' experiences and adapting to the ongoing or evolving needs of the community are key to this element. Key questions to consider before diving into this section:

- What are your library's stated mission and values? Are they related to recent needs assessment findings?
- Did you go through a formal strategic planning process to develop the mission and values and articulate them?

- Can you name one library offering, including goals and objectives, that supports the library's mission or values as stated? Can you name one library offering that does not?

Engage. This component involves communicating directly and effectively to the community we serve. Communication includes messages about the library, our mission, and our offerings. It also includes ongoing communication with our users and feedback about their perceptions, understandings, and experiences of the library. Key questions to consider before diving into this section:

- Does your library regularly review its communication strategy for users, partners, and decision makers in your community?
- Who are your key audiences, and what messages about the library are most compelling to them?
- Does your library have an identifiable "brand"? What components of the brand can you identify, and how are they used?
- What messages and tactics does your library currently employ or want to experiment with?

Iterate. Evaluation is the key to understanding how well we're doing in our aims to identify and meet our users' needs. From "good faith" and "library standards," assessing and iterating library services so that they are more relevant has now turned to the impacts or outcomes of our services on the communities we serve. This component includes return on investment and case studies that demonstrate specific impacts. Key questions to consider before diving into this section:

- Has your library formally evaluated a specific service or offering? What were the service's goals and intended outcomes, and how were they implemented?
- Did the program reach its goals? What were the outcomes?
- What are your library's standard evaluation methods? What tools do you use, and how are findings analyzed?
- Have you ever been surprised by your evaluation findings? What was one unexpected finding or

recommendation, and what changes did your library make as a result?

Sustain. Considering the medium- and long-term implications of our services is key to what some have called "future-proofing" the library. In short, you want to stay feasible, flexible, and adaptable so that library services stay relevant and are always meeting needs, in an ongoing fashion. Key questions to consider before diving into this section:

- Does your library regularly evaluate, plan for, and implement change? In what ways?
- How does sustainability factor into your library's decision-making process?
- Do programs include internal mechanisms for supporting themselves after development and initial implementation?
- How do you sustain your work as a library professional? How do you stay engaged with others working in libraries?

Our project never set out to produce a community-building formula, recipe, or how-to guide. Steven and I simply sought to offer a theoretical and contextual framework for building community through libraries, collect insights from contemporary library staff about their roles and projects building community through libraries, and wherever possible share the specific stories and projects of the library staff we talked with in their own words. But along the way we also uncovered a few conceptual trends that we felt worth further exploration and consideration, and these are outlined in the afterword.

LIBRARIES BUILD COMMUNITIES: THE PROJECT

Perhaps serendipitously, Steven and I pulled the principles we discovered library staff were using to build communities locally into the project as a whole. First, we set up a blog and website at http://libraries buildcommunities.org (LBC) to get the project started and engage our colleagues in our questions and ideas, both initially and ongoing. Our survey of library staff was conducted online, and we published our findings and excerpts from the manuscript on the LBC site as well. We also hosted a number of meet-ups and after-hours get-togethers at library conferences and meetings, and conducted one-on-one interviews with library staff in person, through e-mail, and by phone.

Throughout each chapter, text boxes tell more thorough stories in the contributor's own voice and often include contact or additional resource information. Throughout this discovery and retelling, I've struggled to keep the stories of the library workers from being encumbered by my own ideas or boiled down into a strict list of strategies or a step-by-step process. On the other hand, I've tried to extract a concentrated set of concepts that are easy to understand and that are very practicable. This has required a delicate balance, and I'm sure you will find my attempts more successful in some places than in others.

Some of the stories focus on one component of community building, others on several. Some projects were ultimately successful in all components examined, others in only a few. These stories, along with our research, have framed the questions we invite you to consider as you continue to move your library toward community-centered practice. Ultimately, there is no magical or truly "future-proof" recommendation that we can offer you for developing community through libraries. In spite of our efforts to uncover what can be learned from all these experiences, community building remains an art.

I am frequently speaking (in person) and hosting ongoing conversations (in person and online) about libraries and community building. The site at http://librariesbuildcommunities.org will stay active as long as there's continued interest in the topic—please visit me online to join the discussion, or visit the meet-ups page to see if we'll be in the same place any time soon.

EXCERPTS FROM THE LANDSCAPE

Many of the library staff we talked to gave us snapshots of their careers, libraries, or special community-building projects. These stories have been placed in highlighted areas throughout the chapters. Following is a complete list of the text boxes and the chapters in which they appear.

Assess

FIND THE NEEDS, FILL THE LIBRARY—Rachel MacNeilly, Mission Branch, San Francisco Public Library, California

UNDERSTANDING URBAN IMMIGRANT COMMUNITIES—Valerie Wonder, Seattle Public Library, Washington

DRIVING DECISIONS WITH DATA—Marlena Boggs, Mid-Continent Public Library, Independence, Missouri

CHINESE STORYTELLERS EXPAND SUMMER READING—Valerie Wonder, Seattle Public Library, Washington

Deliver

DISCURSIVE DESIGN—Jeff Scott, City of Casa Grande Public Library, Arizona

MEANING, NOT MATERIALS—Steven Bell, Temple University, Pennsylvania

TEENLINKS HOOKS TEENS INTO LIBRARY SERVICES—Meg Canada,Hennepin County Library, Minneapolis, Minnesota

PARTNER IS POWER—Cheryl Napsha, Bethel Park Public Library, Pennsylvania

Engage

MARKETING BUILDS COMMUNITIES—Jill Stover, James Branch Cabell Library, Virginia Commonwealth University

PUTTING PATRONS ON THE MAP—Molly Rodgers, Wayne County Public Library, Pennsylvania

UN-MARKETING—Michael Porter, WebJunction.org

Iterate

HELPING LIBRARIES DEMONSTRATE IMPACT—Joanne Roukens, Highlands Regional Library Cooperative, New Jersey

EVALUATION BUILDS COMMUNITIES—Catherine D'Italia, Hartford Public Library, Connecticut

SUSTAINABLE OUTCOMES—Christopher Jowaisas, Texas State Library

Sustain

NOTHING IS IMPOSSIBLE—Cynthia Fuerst, Kankakee Public Library, Illinois

SUSTAINING RURAL LIBRARIES—Cindi Hickey, State Library of Kansas, and Brenda Hough, Northeast Kansas Library System

FRIENDS GROUPS HELP WITH FUNDING—Rebekkah Smith Aldrich, Mid-Hudson Library System, New York

BLOGS BUILD COMMUNITY (WITH PEOPLE I SEE EVERY DAY)— Helene Blowers, Columbus Metropolitan Library, Ohio

FIVE WEEKS TO A SOCIAL LIBRARY—Meredith Farkas, Information Wants to Be Free (blog)

CHAPTER THREE

Assess

To varied individual needs, the Library Staff must attend with equal efficiency.
—S. R. Ranganathan, *Five Laws of Library Science,* 1931

Criteria for community building are (1) understand community information
needs, (2) analyze the needs and generate options, (3) identify solutions
based on the best possible alternative, (4) inform all the stakeholders . . .
—Koteswara Tumuluru, Technical Library, Chennai, India

LIBRARIANS (DON'T ALWAYS) KNOW BEST

"Libraries are about service, or they are about nothing"

HISTORIANS OF LIBRARY PRACTICE INDICATE that our early values reflected the mores and trends of the time. In *Foundations of Library and
Information Science,* for example, Richard Rubin examines the history of
library missions, beginning with records archiving. Subsequent library missions have included religion, scholarship, research, personal status, public
use, and national pride. In the United States, as libraries developed up to
the nineteenth century, types included self-improvement "social" libraries, mass appeal "circulating" libraries, commercial-profit "business" libraries, teaching and research "academic" libraries, and educational "school"
libraries that supported curriculum. The social and the circulating libraries
joined in the early American public library's general mission: to serve the
public (Rubin 2004).

Still, qualifications for "serving the public" were subjective and sometimes determined by prevalent morals or perspectives. In *The Politics
of an Emerging Profession,* Wayne Wiegand notes that librarians of the
newly formed American Library Association believed that the public was

"generally incapable of choosing its own reading material judiciously." Their role, then, was to "intervene for the benefit of society" by "acquiring and prescribing the best reading materials for the reading public's consumption" (Wiegand 1986, 230). In other words, if libraries were to "uplift" their communities, librarians and other "apostles of culture" knew best how to do it. Early collections focused on positive values like thrift, sportsmanship, and citizenship, and service was sprinkled with "missionary zeal" (Augst 2001, 12).

By the 1920s and 1930s, important shifts were taking place in the profession, including the addition of large numbers of paid, women professionals and, perhaps along with them, the opening of stacks, the founding of youth service, and provision of services to immigrants. In all, a shift from cultural uplift to community-based services took place through the mid-twentieth century (McCook 2004).

In spite of our early history of favoring collections and expertise over service, foundation texts never fail to remind us that service is central to the tenets of our profession. In fact, our profession has an indelible history of service commitment and values. Ranganathan's *Five Laws of Library Science,* published in 1931, focused on professional library services to all people rather than on collections management for preservation's sake or to serve library staff interests. Looking at the five laws now (see the text box "Five Laws Focus on Library Service"), we see not only their influence on twentieth-century libraries but also their relevance to contemporary library practice. Decades later, Pierce Butler characterized "the cultural motivation of librarianship" as "the promotion of wisdom in the individual and the community . . . to communicate, so far as possible, the whole of scholarship to the whole community" (1951, 246–47). And Michael Gorman, with his update to Ranganathan's laws more than a half century later, noted that the "dominant ethic" of librarianship is "service to the individual, community, and society as a whole. . . . Libraries are about service, or they are about nothing" (1995, 1998).

Community-focused library practice is not new. Yet, when Ruth Warncke published *Analyzing Your Community: Basis for Building Library Service* for the Illinois Library Association and the Illinois State Library in 1974, it was because she and her colleagues had realized that community needs were essential to library services but still missing from public library planning. In fact, the state had recently set out to develop and implement public library standards across Illinois, and its first laudable step was goal setting. "The board and the staff should jointly accept the responsibility of developing objectives and goals," the state had said, "tailored to meet

FIVE LAWS FOCUS ON LIBRARY SERVICE

Ranganathan's Five Laws of Library Science (1931)

- Books are for use [not for storage or preservation].
- Books are for all [everyone should have access].
- Every book his reader [someone wants to read it].
- Save the time of the reader [provide timely, efficient services].
- The library is a living organism [we must grow in order to survive].

Gorman's Five "New Laws" of Librarianship (1995)

- Libraries serve humanity.
- Protect free access to knowledge.
- Respect all forms by which knowledge is communicated [an upgrade from books and readers alone].
- Use technology intelligently to enhance service [where relevant to the library's mission].
- Honor the past and create the future [focus on new information and preservation of the cultural record].

the needs of the individual community." As with most plans, once you get in there and get started, you realize what you don't know. "Most of us," reflected Jean Baron, chair of the committee, "no matter how well we think we know our communities, need to know more" (Warncke 1974, iv).

Along with Warncke, Margaret Monroe championed the inclusion of reliable, documented understanding of the community to inform library practice and to improve the services we were intent on providing. In her final work, *Memoirs of a Public Librarian* (2006), Monroe shares her vision "of what a public library should be," as it developed over the course of a career in library service. Her vision was a composite of all the public libraries she had worked with, including New York Public, Detroit, Denver, Philadelphia, Boston, Andover, and Enoch Pratt Free Library in Baltimore, which together had developed a shared public library service style across the United States. In short, they all focused on "bringing information to bear on human problems and community issues," with an increased focus on problem solving with their communities.

Since the 1970s, community needs assessment has been present, but not prevalent, in library practice. Between 1979 and the present, 193 library-related needs assessment publications have been cataloged in WorldCat. Many of these describe local community assessment projects that identified needs and related library services in specific geographic areas or for specific population targets. Few resources exist that focus exclusively on assisting library staff with the process and methods of needs assessments where the desired outcome is improved or new library services. Yet many of the librarians Steven and I spoke to throughout our research indicated that community needs were top of mind for community-building librarians. They were consistently asking, in one way or another, "How can I find out what is really happening in my community?" Following are some of their comments on the importance of understanding community needs.

> Our goals are to be there for the community, to serve their needs and be responsive to their requests. (Melissa Willer, Bloomingdale Public Library, Illinois)
>
> • • •
>
> I often hear myself asking people "who's the audience?" for a service, collection, program . . . which helps to focus attention on the clients rather than the collections. (Mylee Joseph, State Library of New South Wales, Australia)
>
> • • •
>
> The total population of our city and township is 3,000. . . . We must be responsive to our community or our patrons will go to neighboring communities where they already grocery shop, go to doctors, and work. Because our community is a vacation area, we deal with two factions. We have a year-round population that tends to be much more poor and less educated than the wealthy people from Chicago who summer here. Currently, our community is being challenged by the different needs and wants of the two groups. In our last planning cycle, the library was mentioned again and again as a place of peace and mutual support by both. . . . This is because we manage to balance the needs of the two groups

well and are both listening and responsive to all. (Tasha Saecker, Caestecker Public Library, Green Lake, Wisconsin)

• • •

Treat each library member as an individual with distinctive needs. Always ask questions. (Angela Tuson, ITEC Community Library, East London, South Africa)

• • •

[Community building] is a matter of training, changing skill sets, and understanding the role library staff members play. We need to change the way we think about the library to reflect current culture and trends. We need to go to where the people are and "make" them our patrons. We cannot sit idly by waiting for them to come and use the materials that we have so diligently "collected." We must change our perspective to meet their changing needs. (Stephen Territo, Vernon Area Public Library District, Lincolnshire, Illinois)

• • •

Our library's mission includes the goals for teaching information literacy and intellectual property throughout the community that we serve (students, faculty, and staff) and to provide services that match the needs of patrons and that are current with the best practices in our profession. (Mark McCallon, Abilene Christian University, Texas)

• • •

We come at community building as a user-centered library, trying to identify and meet the needs of the long tail of niche user markets. Community building is our way of bringing the library to the users. (Victor Liu, Washtenaw Community College Library, Ann Arbor, Michigan)

• • •

[Community building] is about what your community tells you it needs, which they may not say explicitly. For instance, when we researched community organizations, they all told us they were fine with the library, but that they needed help staying more in touch with other organizations. They didn't think of us as having a role in networking. We realized they couldn't tell us what they needed from us because they didn't know what we could do, or what we were capable of. It was less useful to ask them if they liked us and more useful to ask them what kinds of problems they were having. (Steve Backs, Monroe County Public Library, Bloomington, Indiana)

Across the globe, and in multiple types of libraries and various professional roles, library staff who view the profession through a community-building lens value customer needs and express the importance of allocating time and resources toward understanding them. Still, it can be difficult to know where to start. The following section can be used as a guide to community needs assessment and provides some examples of libraries using various methods to understand needs in their community for better library service.

FIND THE NEEDS, FILL THE LIBRARY
A public library branch visit with Rachel MacNeilly

Rachel MacNeilly is the children's services manager at the Mission Branch of the San Francisco Public Library. I had heard from a colleague that she runs a bilingual lapsit program twice each Thursday, with an average of 120 people in attendance *every* session. When I arrived at the library, I was greeted by thirty to fifty strollers parked outside the library and then arranged in a single line through the hallway to the children's area. The room was crowded with kids and their caregivers talking, laughing, and trying to get a place up front. When I met Rachel, I understood the force she had become in her library and her community. "I live in this neighborhood," Rachel told me. "These kids can't hide from me for long. They *will* come to storytime." In less than one year, Rachel has changed children's programming from a single session once a week with an average of forty-five attendees to multiple programs per week and almost five times the attendees. How did she do it?

First, she assessed the needs and patterns of use of the patron base that already existed at the branch. She found that patrons were attending programs and promptly leaving the facility afterward without a second thought of reading on their own. She also found that the standard storytime offerings were not engaging the patrons in the neighborhood. By asking many patrons many questions, she was able to get a clearer idea of their literacy needs and wishes. She hoped to incorporate these needs and wants into a really engaging programming event. Her investigation resulted in major scheduling shake-ups at the branch. The number of programs for infants and children up to age 3 rose from one to three per week, and each storytime is designed to include both English and Spanish songs and rhymes. The format became much more interactive and includes movement with scarves and rhythm with cluster bells, egg shakers, and rhythm sticks, and emphasizes to adults the importance of positive interaction with their little ones. The results have been dramatic, with adults and children staying in the library for hours after the program to read and to interact with other babies and their grownups. The atmosphere has morphed from a traditional, formal experience to a more community-based and relaxed experience that welcomes people to feel at home in the space.

Second, Rachel did some weeding of the collection in her library. "I want this place to look like Nordstrom, *not* the Nordstrom Rack!" she beams. And it worked using the following principle: she allows no children's materials in the library that are "older than me" or that look "junky." "I got rid of everything that looked awful," Rachel said, and the funny thing is that "with less on the shelves, there's less on the shelves" (meaning that people check things out more). Circulation has almost doubled, but it's still not up to where she'd like it to be; she has aggressive goals for upping her circulation stats in the coming year, stats that match what she's been able to do with the program stats. "I love stats," Rachel said. "You can think you're changing things, but stats let you know if you really are."

Rachel's impact on the programming attendance in her library is directly related to the facts that programs are bilingual, they are offered at appropriate times of day for their intended audiences, and they have benefited from a complete and recent overhaul of the content. Content is more age appropriate and more focused on touch and movement. "I also add practical information to storytime for the caregivers," noted Rachel. "Every hour I do a program,

I give them a development tip that I hope they will find really helpful."

During my visit, I was awestruck by the energy and emotion in the fully packed, standing-room-only, one-hour bilingual program. When I asked her about online community building, Rachel told me that she's begun a website just for her branch. The site is accessible to both English-speaking and Spanish-speaking patrons and allows them to access all the storytime content, songs, and calendar of events in both English and Spanish. "My patrons are busy," Rachel said. "They don't have time to search for numbers and call the branch." The process of building the site was rocky, but Rachel claims it was worth the trouble. Once patrons learned that they would be able to listen to storytime songs and rhymes online, their excitement really started to build. The content highlights the branch's wonderful array of storytimes and opportunities for parents/caregivers and children to share the joy of reading books and exploring print. Because so many of the regulars at storytime at the library are caregivers, the website's links to songs and rhymes will allow parents at home to participate in their child's exploration of literacy. So far, the site has a blog component, a calendar of events, audio tracks to the songs from storytime with each song's words printed, information about developmental milestones, and a list of community support agencies for the neighborhood. When I asked Rachel what makes her programs and services so successful, especially in so short a time, she said very simply, "My people ask me for what they need, and I just try to get it for them."

It's just that simple.

Rachel MacNeilly is the children's services manager at the San Francisco Public Library's Mission Branch. Her website is http://missionkidsread.org, where new content goes up every day.

COMMUNITY NEEDS ASSESSMENT

"No matter how well we think we know, we need to know more"

Libraries operate in an increasingly complex environment. Changing neighborhoods and lifestyles, local economies, shifting demographics, and trends in policy or funding all influence the services we deliver and the people we serve. And although our professional history and values often assist us in making decisions about what to offer and where to evolve, many library services are delivered without detailed or documented information about our communities or their needs.

Community needs analysis begins with a definition of *needs* and *wants*. *Needs* are items that, when supplied, fill the gap between a desired condition and a current condition—they help meet a goal. *Wants* are desired, but don't fill the gap or meet the goal. A formal needs assessment can frame the problems or opportunities in a community, and build relationships among the people or organizations that are stakeholders in meeting those needs. Needs analysis also provides the foundation for planning. It guides and informs the actions required to meet needs by further clarifying opportunities, aligning resources with strategy, setting goals for future action, and supporting decision making with real data. (For more on the basics from the training and development perspective, see Gupta, Sleezer, and Russ-Eft 2007.) A comprehensive needs assessment will provide information about a defined population, whether bound by geography, role, or status. It will also provide a description of the needs of the population as well as an inventory of existing services or resources. Finally, a gap analysis of met and unmet needs is outlined, prioritized, and presented so that it can be used for future planning and decision making.

If you're doing a community needs assessment, start by answering the following questions, adapted from a basic needs and assets assessment worksheet presented in a March 2006 workshop called Promoting Public Libraries: Using Data and Advocacy to Build Public Support and Funding (Gates Foundation 2006). These questions will not only get you thinking but also outline the process for implementing and using a needs assessment.

- What is your library's needs and assets assessment goal?
- Which populations do you want to learn more about?
- What data already exist?
- What original data will you collect?
- How will you collect information?
- What are your library's existing assets to help meet the needs of your target populations?
- What are your library's primary barriers to meeting the needs of your target populations?
- What type of information do you need to collect to meet the needs of your community?
- Who will work together to conduct this study?
- How will you use the information you collect?

Next we'll look in depth at each of these questions.

UNDERSTANDING URBAN IMMIGRANT COMMUNITIES

By Valerie Wonder

The Seattle Public Library (SPL) is a twenty-six-branch system with a large central library serving a diverse community of 550,000. With a Literacy, ESL, and World Languages Department located in the central library, and collections of non-English materials at strategically located "magnet" branches throughout the system, the library has had a long-standing tradition of serving immigrants and refugees. But in 2000, City Librarian Deborah Jacobs appointed a staff committee to explore how to further enhance our services to these communities. This initial group expanded into a task force that broadened our services and provided organizational involvement. On the basis of these early efforts, the Seattle Public Library Foundation secured funding to support current and ongoing library services to immigrants and refugees, including the creation of my current position.

A key component of our service planning was to begin with a single community and then expand to other immigrant and refugee communities. We began our efforts with the Spanish-speaking community and are now broadening our work to include other language groups based on population density. In 2003 the task force did a comprehensive study of the Spanish-speaking community in Seattle. They asked such questions as: Who makes up this community? What agencies serve and/or represent the residents? What churches, schools, and businesses do Spanish speakers use? What needs exist? How have Spanish speakers been served by SPL in the past? How could this service improve?

Research lasted a year and included a review of relevant resources followed by interviews and focus groups with library staff, community agencies, and library patrons. Resulting recommendations led to our current programs and services, which include traditional library programs offered in Spanish as well as new programs, such as Spanish-language workshops on credit, loan acquisition, or citizenship. We revisit these questions regularly to make adjustments to our approach to serving this diverse community.

We are now broadening our work to include other language groups based on population density and are following a similar approach. By working methodically and forming deep connections within each community, we have been able to assess, make changes, and evaluate this work while continuing to bring new users to our library.

Valerie Wonder is the Immigrant and Refugee Programs manager for the Seattle Public Library, where she develops cultural and life skills programs for immigrant communities. Her work with Chinese-speaking communities in Seattle is described later in this chapter.

As you articulate your goals for conducting the needs assessment, also ask, "Whose needs will the project address?" and "What do we already know?" For example, if your goal is to improve staff training or development, you may be interested in staff as a target community within your library. You may be interested in your entire public, research, or department community, or in your institution's specific service population such as students, faculty, teachers, or employees. In any case, basic information about your target group is likely available. The size of the population, the organization of the governing agency, supporting service agency names, the organization and populations of related schools, the number and types of churches, and the demographic characteristics of your population or target groups within it should all be available. The most obvious place to start is with existing library staff or users within the target community, which we could also call our core market. Regular users might be qualified by a general interest in building knowledge, learning, or exploring, by their understanding of the library, our services, and organization, or by their desire to access the types of materials or services libraries already offer. One mistake, however, is to focus only on existing users. For a thorough community needs analysis, it's important to look beyond regular library users to those on the fringe of our market, and beyond them to nonusers. Marylaine Block's *The Thriving Library* (2007) includes a full chapter with case studies on nontraditional users and how to reach them. In every case, we are seeking to understand needs in order to better serve our whole community.

Library staff and organization needs also come into play. Any available details should be gathered about staff skills, interests, or expertise as well as about the library's income, expenditures, organization, programs, circulation, partnerships, Friends groups, and trustees. Previous library surveys or focus group findings, suggestions or complaint records, national library data, data collected from other agencies, and literature reviews (local and national) can all be accessed to build the profiles of your library and community. And as you venture into community profiling, it can help to stay in tune with local concerns, issues, or events by reading, listening to, and watching local media or attending local meetings. Joining or otherwise participating in local organizations can also help you keep your fingers on the pulse of your community. Regularly attending local festivals, events, and other community gatherings can provide more information about community needs or interests. Conducting needs assessment in the context of the social network within which the library will operate and grow is an ongoing task, but you can't build your community without starting here.

DRIVING DECISIONS WITH DATA

Quantitative information helps the Mid-Continent Public Library in Missouri precisely identify community needs.

Tell us about your library and the community you serve.

Our library's mission is to "provide expanding access to materials, programs, [and] technology . . . by ensuring the highest quality staff meeting the wants and needs of diverse populations." We have thirty branches in three counties, serving approximately 600,000 people. After I had spent several years as a manager for one of our larger branches, our library board created my current position and gave me three mandates: do more programming; work with literacy; work with and in the community.

How does your library identify community needs?

In 2005 we were finally able to subscribe to the Claritas databases, which provide for segmentation. (Especially helpful in defining our community has been the MyBestSegments database.) Using this database, we can pinpoint which branches serve which parts of our community. Claritas takes not only the census information but also information from Nielsen and other research firms and then aggregates all the data into reports on everything from which magazines the segments read to which cereal they tend to eat. We use the Sirsi system and are now associating the information from our patrons with library cards to the segments that they are in.

How has this information been used to inform library services?

This information has allowed us to not just pick programs we *think* will fit our patrons, but that we *know* are going to fulfill a need.

Marlena Boggs is the adult specialist at the Mid-Continent Public Library (MCPL) in Independence, Missouri. MCPL is online at www.mcpl.lib.mo.us.

With your targets identified, along with what's already known about them, it's time to start tackling what you don't know. Now we have to identify the information gaps for target groups. Brainstorming answers to the question, What do we not know? can start this list of important questions. Prioritizing these questions for potential further inquiry can be done by relative importance, immediacy or timeliness, the ability to get results quickly or easily, or the ability to answer (at all). When in doubt, the library's stated mission or purpose should help keep the process focused and relevant. In this stage, you'll be doing new or original research based on the background you've built thus far. Your research may seek to uncover key issues, such as what matters to your targets. You might also seek to further detail the characteristics of the library or your targets, such as how users access the service, when, and how often. You may even delve into what works and what doesn't. Predictive research or scenario planning might indicate "what happens if . . . ?" This type of research can be used to explore new materials formats, operating hours, or special program offerings. You might also seek feedback about how the library can improve, what services or programs the library should consider, how satisfied current users or nonusers are with the library, how much they understand the library, or what might be missing from existing library services. Several methods are available for conducting this type of research. The key is finding the right method for your needs and resources. A few examples follow.

Individual surveys can be conducted randomly or with targets in the library or out in the community. Some libraries choose to work with a research firm, purchase data, or use geographic information systems or demographic databases to acquire information they don't already have access to. The Mid-Continent Public Library, for example, shared with me how their use of the Claritas database helps them identify who lives in their service area and what those residents' needs may be. Interviews can also be conducted with representative community members, leaders, or members of various groups. WebJunction's Spanish Language Outreach Project provides an excellent guide for conducting interviews with key community leaders. The Carnegie Library of Pittsburgh partnered with the design firm MAYA to conduct a usability study of the library from the perspective of the customers' experience with facilities, systems, and staff. The resulting full-scale redesign of the library left users stunned. "This is the coolest thing I have ever seen ever in a library," said one patron. "I am going to hug the librarian," said another. "If I could hug the whole library I would."[1] Other research methods include building case studies, examining customer use patterns, conducting online or in-person surveys, performing desk research, forming focus groups, doing community profiling, and even engaging mystery shoppers (Kendrick 2006).

As a result of your research, you'll now have more accurate, documented information about target segments and their interests, concerns, and personal needs as well as about community problems, concerns, or priorities. This information can set a baseline for future evaluation of your ongoing library services. You'll be able to track and report on your library's ability to respond to and meet the needs you identified if you know where you're starting from.

CHINESE STORYTELLERS EXPAND SUMMER READING

With Valerie Wonder

The immigrant populations in Seattle are extremely diverse in experiences and needs, but all share a deep desire to give their children opportunities for education and success. It is that desire that leads many immigrant families to the library for the first time. What better way to serve immigrant needs *and* make deep connections in communities than to create opportunities for non-English-speaking children while reaching out to their parents?

As in many libraries, our summer reading program is the system's largest and most well attended. However, children who speak a language other than English at home are proportionally underrepresented among participants. To address this I'm working closely with our Youth Program manager to pilot a Chinese Language Storytime. If the program is successful, we will expand it to Spanish and Vietnamese speakers.

To build a pool of qualified Chinese-speaking storytellers and build support from library personnel, we teamed up with the Children's Department and enlisted the help of our Chinese-speaking children's librarian to create a training session and develop a series of "storytimes in a box" kits that new storytellers may use for their programs. This approach ensures that story-tellers learn the basic principles of early literacy and storytime techniques and are exposed to our library staff and collections. To further ensure success we recruited native Chinese speakers who have experience working with youth and in libraries.

This summer our trained storytellers will offer sixteen Chinese Storytimes in four branches that house Chinese collections and serve Chinese speakers locally. Children's librarians at each branch will be on hand to answer questions, sign up families for library cards, highlight items from the collection, and develop relationships with parents and youth. We will also use this as an opportunity to solicit feedback and ideas for future programming and to make Chinese-language community information available. To promote the storytimes, we will use Chinese-language fliers and advertise through Chinese newspapers and radio stations, but more important we are building partnerships with key community-based organizations that will bring groups of parents and children to the programs.

Our library measures the success of all our programs on the following factors: attracting new users to the library, educating program participants about other relevant library services, whether participants enjoy the program, potential for community building, and cost-effectiveness. Initial evaluation of this pilot will be done through librarian surveys, storyteller surveys, participation data, and translated parent surveys. So far, the community response has been overwhelmingly positive. Staff have been slightly more cautious, thoughtfully probing for information about the program's sustainability and for confirmation that quality will be upheld and community connections captured—but are now very supportive of this effort to expand their reach into the community.

Valerie Wonder is the Immigrant and Refugee Programs manager for the Seattle Public Library, where she develops cultural and life skills programs for immigrant communities.

One obstacle that can hinder the needs assessment process or the implementation of needs assessment findings is the decision making that must take place as a result. In a recent survey of library innovators, respondents asked explicitly that their library directors and managers "make decisions faster" in order to support change, growth, and innovations (or just get to the daily routine, in some cases; Hill 2008). It can be tough to make a decision not to continue to "cover the waterfront," especially when our service or social values are to be all-inclusive. There are a lot of good ideas, a lot of things we could do, and a lot of things that are important in their own rights, but don't necessarily point to crucial needs. If we avoid critical implications produced by the assessment research and analysis, we'll continue to provide irrelevant or partially relevant services, or continue to do a mediocre job across a number of services when attention would be better spent on meeting one or two vital needs and meeting them well. Prioritizing options and moving plans forward immediately will quickly engage your library staff colleagues, your assessment committee, and the community at large.

In spite of its particular importance in ensuring that library services remain relevant, needs assessment remains supplemental for most library practitioners. Aside from a few state library agencies that have conducted and published statewide needs assessments relative to library services, along with the examples in this chapter, community needs assessment is not prevalent in our service delivery models. However, as I've looked into the community needs assessment work that librarians have shared with me, I've recognized that behind all their work is the importance of building relationships, a fact certainly central to libraries building communities. These library staff started by asking people in the library and the community to get involved with the needs assessment project. When others participate, they may be more likely to understand the questions that the library seeks to answer, understand the findings, and see to it that the implications of the assessment are met with some kind of service response. For everyone from nonusers to community leaders and stakeholders, segment knowledge holders, researchers, marketing consultants, designers, data and number crunchers, library Friends, trustees, regular users, and staff—their involvement in the needs assessment process builds a relationship you can leverage later for outreach and service implementation.

Ongoing communications and relationships with our community leaders are invaluable. And whether we're seeking to gain insights into a new demographic group like Spanish speakers or a new special interest group like knitters or gamers, it helps to know who the leaders are and to stay in close contact with them. I have also noticed that these librarians talk about getting out from behind their desks and even outside the library and into the communities they aim to serve. Taking part in meetings, serving on civic boards, taking leadership or participatory roles in community organizations, showing up for community events, and maintaining a consistent presence online all point to new ways that being a librarian takes place outside our facilities and beyond our staff hours. My hopes are that twenty-first-century library practice will approach understanding customer needs in a formalized, structured manner and that more of these studies and experiences will be documented and shared throughout the profession.

NOTE

1. Visit Mid-Continent Public Library at www.mcpl.lib.mo.us for links to its mission, strategic plans, and annual report, which outlines some of the ways the library stays in touch with customer needs. WebJunction's Spanish Language Outreach Guide for community leader interviews is at www.webjunction.org/slo-workshop -materials/resources/wjarticles/. Visit http://darmano.typepad .com/for_blog/rettiggoel.uxWeek.8.25.05.pdf for more information on the MAYA redesign of the Carnegie Library of Pittsburgh.

CHAPTER FOUR

Deliver

The best way to build community is to be a part of the community. Go to meetings. Get to know people. Go to anything involving kids—sports, music, theater, whatever it is that kids in your community do. Try to work with people rather than against them. If you have teenagers causing a problem in the library, don't boot them out—ask them what the library could be doing for them, and work together to make it happen.

—Laura Crossett, Branch Manager, Meeteetse Branch Library, Wyoming

LIBRARIES: OUT OF BUSINESS?

"I wish we could call FEMA"

THE FIRST WEEK OF APRIL 2007, the fifteen-branch Jackson County Library System in Medford, Oregon, closed its doors—all of them—due to the projected loss of federal timber subsidies to the county. "I wish I could call FEMA," said Ted Stark, interim library director at the time of the shutdown. "This feels like a natural disaster to me" (May 2007). Five weeks later, in response to the largest library closure in history, according to the American Library Association, a local Save Our Libraries group made up of library staff, volunteers, and local citizens rallied support for a voter levy. If passed, the levy would shift library funding from the federal subsidy source to a local funding source based on increased property taxes. In spite of all fifteen libraries being closed for forty days, the levy was overwhelmingly defeated. "It is always a tough proposition, no matter what the issue," said one local blogger and library supporter, "to ask people who don't have enough money to begin with to raise their own taxes" (Lieberman 2007a). A similar levy was defeated again in November, after the library had been closed for six months. Jackson County eventually reopened its branches, but only after a bidding war between the original employee union and the Maryland-based LSSI (Library Systems and Services, Inc.). LSSI proposed reduced staff benefits, reduced service hours, and a service model dependent on library clerks and volunteers. Mark Smith, the transition leader for LSSI, promised that his company made "every effort to create a library system that offers the same or better level of service as [customers] received previously" (Lieberman 2007b). Librarians everywhere lamented the reduced service level for local citizens and the transfer of county library system operations to a distant, private, for-profit company, but county officials held firm. County Administrator Danny Jordan told *Library Journal* that officials were simply responding when citizens asked (through their defeat of the levy) to "make the system less expensive" (Oder 2007).

Since the broad adoption of Internet access at both home and work, we've heard that libraries were likely to close. Is the library still relevant in a digital age? Stories of public libraries on the brink of extinction like those in Jackson County appeared in Salinas and Merced County, California, in Niagara Falls, New York, in Trenton, New Jersey, and elsewhere. But it's not just the Internet, and it's not just public libraries. At the time of this writing, federal and school libraries were also under greater scrutiny, and for some of the same reasons. Following is an excerpt from a blog entry by a technical information specialist in a federal library, frantically calling for help in defense of his library, with little time to prepare the proof his challengers are looking for.

> Recently, the military has been forced to make some budget cuts, and as is usually the case, the "easy target" library has come under the microscope. We were suddenly and inexplicably placed under a highly aggressive "work group" comprised of lean Six-Sigma-ready business ninjas. They want to close/move/consolidate or minimize our already scant resources. As is always the case, our customers know the value of the library. We've already received official letters, memos, testimonials etc. . . . from a wide range of military historians, commanders, executive officers, and researchers, but it seems to be not enough.
>
> FY06 marked the closings of nationwide EPA libraries, and the Air Force has decided to close all of its medical libraries. We're getting a little freaked out. We must prove to the current bureaucracy that after 171 years, we are still an asset to the organization. We have a plan of attack; we're wearing out a copy of *Making the Case for Your Library*. What we lack is information. That's all this work group wants. Graphs, charts, spreadsheets, and death by

PowerPoint. If we could argue the entire case using ones and ze-ros, we'd be in good shape.

We are hoping that you may have researched or know some-one who has researched the impact of closing a library. We'd like to know the cost differences between reciprocal document delivery and independent research contractors. Physical librarian vs. 100 percent automated databases. The bosses are looking for short-term cost avoidance, and if they can save FY07 funds by canning the library, they won't hesitate. We wouldn't ask you for this if we had time to compile the data, but we don't have time. They want everything immediately. It's like an information ambush: defend your library with some annual usage stats that mean nothing to the work group and a wet noodle. Good luck! (Cornwall 2007)

As this blogger noted, the Environmental Protection Agency closed its libraries in 2007 because of 80 percent budget cuts affecting libraries across the agency. "When libraries go digital," said the EPA spokesper-son, "everyone wins." When resources are tight, the library can become an easy target if decision makers are not library users or supporters, or if the users themselves are not supporters. In the case of the EPA librar-ies, Congress ultimately disagreed with "everyone wins," and President Bush signed a bill later that year bringing back all previously closed li-braries. In Spokane, Washington, where school library media centers faced 50 percent reductions in the hours of ten elementary school li-brarians and the third significant cut to school media centers over four years, three local moms developed a grassroots effort to save their local students from "riding an apple cart on the information highway." After a local defeat (the school board voted to reduce hours anyway), the trio realized that the problem was statewide, as other school districts across Washington were cutting media specialist positions and hours. When they realized that the Federal Way School District cut twenty librarians in 2007, with similar actions in Darrington and Granite Falls, they were inspired to create a statewide campaign for school libraries. With the help of the Washington Library Media Association, posts on Craigslist.org, and reaching out to various media outlets to spread the word, they garnered wide support. Finally, they launched a comprehensive website (www .fundourfuturewashington.org), complete with a blog, research, testimo-nials, and ways to support the cause. "I have jokingly referred to them as the 'Network Moms,'" Keith Lance told *School Library Journal.* "They galvanized parents and other school library advocates in a way that hasn't been done before" (Whelan 2008). Academic and special libraries are also shrinking, collapsing, or converging with other functional areas of their institutions in order to continue services under similar financial reductions.

In each of these cases, a concerted grassroots, community effort emerged to save libraries facing closure or just after they closed. Although lack of funding is almost always the reason that libraries close, beneath the lack of financial support is a belief that libraries are no longer relevant in the digital age. There is also the perception that libraries are inefficiently operated or that they lack the services that users need or want most. In reality, little research exists on public or other library closings. In a political or economic climate in which libraries must defend their budgets, status, or services to their stakeholders, a deeper understanding of library reductions and closures is more important than ever.

In 2007 and 2008 the American Library Association and OCLC partnered to support research in this area. The study was conducted by researchers at Florida State University, and their report, "Why Public Libraries Close," is the first systematic look at public library closure on a national basis (Koontz, Jue, and Bishop 2008). Between 1999 and 2003, the number of libraries permanently or temporarily closed in the study's sample was 134 and 105, respectively. Of the libraries studied, "lack of use" was by far the most frequent reason for permanent closure without replacement. Often, according to the researchers, no Internet and no computers were mentioned as reasons that led to a lack of use. Of the 134 permanent library closings, no action was taken in 66 percent of cases. Sometimes the libraries had no ability to take action, but in other instances, the librarians felt there was no need for action. Bookmobile or other outreach services were extended to areas of a permanent closure in only 17 percent of cases; increased programs and services at other library locations occurred in only five instances.

The researchers also studied the impacts of these library closures. During the period of the study (1999–2003), the population within the immediately surrounding one-mile radius of the closed library tended to be poorer, less educated, and more likely to rent rather than own a home when compared to the U.S. population as a whole. These characteristics are often associated with lower mobility and fewer alternatives for information access; therefore, where these population characteristics prevail, closures could disproportionately impact potential library users who may need the public library more than most. Additionally, migration to large population centers may be creating problems for rural libraries. These libraries may find it more difficult to replace library staff. The lowered tax base may make it more difficult for rural library facilities to upgrade to and accommodate the latest information technologies. More research is necessary to understand the impacts of library closures more clearly.

Finally, the researchers asked library staff in affected areas for ideas on how to prevent closures from happening. Their answers clearly pointed to neighborhood advocacy, public relations, and prior planning for ongoing sustainability. They pointed to convenient locations, parking, operating hours, attractive buildings, and provision of services and resources that people need and can access. "Small book rooms without computers . . . will not remain open," researchers warned. This should sound familiar. "The very life of a library is in the service given to the people," Ranganathan argued—a pearl of wisdom for library staff seeking to truly meet community needs with the resources and services they deliver (Ranganathan, Aiyer, and Sayers 1931/2006). What we've termed *deliver* is multifaceted. It includes strategic planning, program design and development, and resource management. Although it may seem simplistic to boil these factors down into a single element of community building, chapter 5 will examine each factor in detail and provide practical strategies and examples that we all can apply toward the delivery of community-centered library services.

DISCURSIVE DESIGN

Open discussions drive library services for growing communities in Arizona.

How did you get started in the library profession?

I began working in an archive, the Arizona Historical Foundation, but I got the bug for libraries before then. I have always loved the concept of library as a place. Book lovers could spend hours in comfortable areas reading books. Now computers, technology, and just the need to "hang out" serve the same purpose for computer users, as well as the readers.

Tell us a little about your library.

Our library system currently consists of one library and a bookmobile. We passed a bond in November 2006 to build a new joint-use library (16,000 square feet), to be completed by June 2009. After that, we will use the remaining funds to expand and renovate the existing facility by 4,000 square feet (20,000 square feet total). After that, we plan to prepare for a new main library on the north side of town that will be 25,000 square feet plus (2015). We are a high-use library with 90 percent of the city having a library card. In 2005, we developed a strategic plan with major stakeholders in the community. Our strategic plan and our esquisse process have been extremely successful community-building projects; we just need more of everything right now, including space.

Why do strategic planning?

Initially, we received a grant from the Arizona State Library as part of PLA's Planning for Results program. Our library staff recommended community members for this Planning for Results board. We conducted three open sessions with this board. We had them visualize what their community would look like if it were a utopia. We then broke these ideas down to match up with what the library actually does and can do. Then we selected three service areas that the board wanted the library to work on. In the next session, we demonstrated what the library does currently and how we would change to meet this community's vision. Library staff then met to develop a plan to be approved by the board. It involved all of the library staff and major community members, and in the end we are doing what the community values and prioritizes. Ultimately, the plan resulted in significant increases in usage and efficiency, and placed the library in the forefront of the community.

What library services were created or improved as a result?

One of the biggest and most successful changes that resulted from this program was the establishment of the only adult literacy tutoring program in Pinal County. Workforce development and literacy were two major issues identified in the community through this process. A recent United Way report stated, for example, that literacy and workforce skills are the third-highest concerns in the entire county. We established a tutoring service with one of our librarians (soon to be two) as a master tutor trainer. We also established bookmobile services within the city as a result of the process, as transportation was another of the major issues identified in the final report. We also established a teen group called Students Participating in an Advisory Reading Committee (SPARC), one of the only teen programs available in the city. This led to huge increases in teen usage for our computers and for our collections. Overall, identifying community needs, and responding to community recommendations, led to huge increases in participation and usage. Over the last year, our circulation increased by 17 percent, our walk-in business by 22 percent, our number of borrowers by 20 percent, and our database users by 70 percent! And these are just a few of the quantifiable measures we are now able to report on as a result of our planning process.

What's an esquisse? Why do you think it was so successful?

An esquisse is simply a first sketch or plan. For our esquisse on the new library building, our architect gave the community a blank slate and asked us what we wanted. The local high school board, the library advisory board, library staff, and the community all helped create our new library. As a result of both our strategic planning and the esquisse, the city is adopting the same model of strategic planning and performance-based budgeting.

Do you have any advice for librarians trying to identify community needs?

Have an open discussion. Open discussions with patrons and staff will provide the best feedback and path to great services. I'm always looking for better ways for patrons to give constant feedback about how they feel about the library and what they would like to change. The more you know about their needs, the faster you can provide them with services.

Jeff Scott is the library director for the City of Casa Grande Public Library in Casa Grande, Arizona, and the president of the Pinal County Library Federation, a consortium of thirteen public libraries. Visit his blog at http://gathernodust.blogspot.com. You can review City of Casa Grande Public Library's strategic planning materials at www.casagrandeaz.gov/web/guest/393/.

STRATEGIC PLANNING: KEEP LIBRARY
SERVICES MISSION-FOCUSED

When Steven and I began our research for this project, we set out to uncover the libraries that were taking a proactive rather than reactive approach to the shrinkage and closure challenges facing libraries. The bottom line is that libraries will always find the need to deliver and demonstrate their value to the communities they serve. Although it may feel like we're living in particularly dire times (as I edit these chapters, the economy has literally collapsed around us and libraries appear to be bracing themselves for extreme challenges ahead), libraries have always operated in environments wrought with political, economic, social, and fiscal change. If we stay focused on our users, stakeholders, and their needs, and continually design for them, we'll be better positioned to stay engaged with our communities no matter what's taking place around us.

Strategic planning is a formal process that can help your library make its first and best response to community needs. The term refers to a "disciplined effort to produce fundamental decisions and actions that shape and guide what an organization is, what it does, and why it does it" (Bryson 1995, 88). Think of this response as a continuation of the dialogue initiated through the assessment process. Strategic planning can help libraries identify the services and offerings that already map to existing community needs, or the needs that libraries are in a position to meet because of their unique resources, skills, or capabilities. Next, strategic planning helps libraries clearly articulate their mission and values as they relate to community needs and the unique offerings of the library. Specific goals and objectives to help focus the library's service deliveries and prioritize resources accordingly are also part of the strategic planning process. Finally, strategic planning can help identify necessary or intended resources related to funding, staff roles and responsibilities, project time lines, service offerings, and outreach or communications plans.

A vision statement tells your audience about the future you see for your community and library. Your mission statement describes how you plan to achieve that vision. Strong vision and mission statements are typically short, direct, and emotionally compelling. They describe in just a few words your greatest ambitions for your community and its members, and the library's place in achieving those results. Following are a few examples of mission statements that specifically address community and the library's role there, originally collected by Linda K. Wallace in *Libraries, Mission, and Marketing: Writing Mission Statements That Work* (2004).

> The Mission of the Daytona State College Library is to encourage, facilitate, and sustain learning for the College Community. (www .daytonastate.edu/library/)

This community college library promotes its mission statement right on its home page.

> The Camden Public Library is a cultural and intellectual center for the community. It provides, at a reasonable cost and in a friendly atmosphere, universal access to knowledge and lifelong learning through print, electronic resources, cultural activities, programs, and services. The library collaborates with other community groups to meet the educational, informational, and recreational needs of the entire community. (www.camden.lib.me.us)

Camden's library mission is easily reached through the prominent "About the Library" link on the library's home page, which also features a friendly welcome to personally support the library with an online donation: "More than 130,000 people visit the Camden Public Library each year. . . . It is both our honor and responsibility to maintain the library and public landscapes as gathering places for ideas, recreation, information and education. The biggest source of funding for the Camden Public Library is our Annual Appeal."

Once goals and objectives for a specific time frame can be articulated by library management and staff, current collections, programs, services, and spaces must be evaluated for their relevance to the needs identified through the assessment process and validated by the library's vision and mission. Articulating where you are, where you'd like to be, how you plan to get there, and how you will know if you got there may seem a daunting task, but it need not be. Several current library-focused publications are available to assist libraries in developing strategic plans that map library services back to a clearly stated vision and mission and to community needs. Many library strategic plans are also published on library websites.

Once the library's vision and mission are articulated, library staff, resources, and work plans should be allocated accordingly. Often, well-circulated items and well-attended programs can immediately be mapped back to specific, documented needs. This is great, because it means that you can leverage what you already have to meet a need that's now even better understood. And while the continued value of these offerings may seem like no-brainers, you must consider and attend to each of them in order to check your assumptions and status quo. Regularly validating even your existing, popular services will allow you to flex and adapt when it's time to improve or even discontinue those services. Decisions to improve one program and discontinue another are difficult and sometimes even avoided. It's easy to slip into "we've always done it this way" or to get attached to "the way things were." No matter how committed, energetic, or innovative library staff are, robust arguments backed by needs-based analysis will keep you clear and intentional about the nature of your work and its intended outcomes. And if analysis of assessment data has outlined specific areas of need or even communities that are not being served already, library staff must be critical of and open about where their current services fall short and be willing to dig into an entirely new service, subject area, or program to make the connections necessary to fill that gap. Change of this magnitude may be difficult to approach and initiate, but think of the alternative. Change and growth to meet patrons and communities as they change and grow is the key to relevant library services, and to the library as the center of your community. As mentioned elsewhere in this book, *The New Planning for Results* (Nelson 2001) offers a streamlined approach to strategic planning that can ensure your library is managing its resources wisely to meet real community needs.

MEANING, NOT MATERIALS
An interview with Steven Bell on experience design for libraries

Why do you think experience design is important for libraries?

I believe that many of our library and nonlibrary users are looking for more meaning in their information seeking and retrieval tasks. Maybe not everyone, but many of them want to be a part of the community we are building—and we can grow it by designing a better library experience. If we look at the ways in which retailers and other service industries are competing for their share of the market, we'll see that many organizations are designing user experiences. So why are they doing this? It's about giving consumers a reason to make a conscious decision to patronize one business instead of another. Let's face it. Libraries are in competition with other providers of information. The people we want to serve can get information anywhere—or they believe they can. We know that most individuals turn to Internet resources first when they need information. Libraries can no longer compete solely on providing access to information or promoting themselves as information gateways; that model is no longer sufficient to grow a user community—if it ever was. Experience design is based on developing meaningful relationships with library users. It is up to each library to decide how to best design that particular type of experience. I will say that some experts have said that you can't design a user experience, you can only create the circumstances and environment in which great experiences can happen. To me that is somewhat the same thing. What I take away from the experts is that it is important to think about and plan great library user experiences, and I think we can do this if we put our energy into the design process.

Do you think design should influence every aspect of library services?

Simply put, my answer is yes. I think it has to because of the concept of the totality of the user experience. I've come to believe that delivering a good user experience is more than just what some experts refer to as the Wow! experience, which is something that greatly impresses the customer. Although those kinds of experiences are great, and I believe that librarians are capable of delivering unexpected great experiences to their communities, a user experience needs to be designed to encompass the totality of the library organization. In other words, if I have a great experience at the circulation desk and then the reference librarian ignores me or treats me indifferently, then I haven't had a good user experience. In fact, I may never come back. Technical services staff are not exempt. Interfaces, systems, and content all have to be considered part of the experience. If it's something your user community comes in contact with, it needs to be considered in the design of the user experience. Do I think this will be easy for libraries? Not at all. But if we want to compete successfully with the Internet and build our community of loyal users, then we have to take on this challenge.

What are some simple things that library managers can do to bring design principles into their practice?

I think the first simple thing they can do is to better understand the meaning of design in a planning process context. For most librarians, design has primarily been about building exteriors and interiors. So the profession needs to expand its understanding of design. One way I like to explain it is that design is approaching library problems the way that designers approach their problems. That means we need to learn how to first understand our users and their needs before we make any effort to develop solutions— and we especially need to be careful not to employ technologies that strike us as solutions, but for which we have no identifiable problem. Library managers can begin by simply bringing up the idea of the user experience in their next staff meeting. Whenever I give workshops on these topics, I am asked for practical library examples. Right now, because this is all so new to the profession, there aren't many good examples. Currently, I look to the business literature to demonstrate to librarians how a design approach can make a difference. I look forward to a time when I'll be able to point to many more examples of how libraries are designing user experiences for their communities, and growing them as a result of this change in how we connect with our communities.

Steven Bell is the associate university librarian for research and instructional services at Temple University. He's the coauthor of and writes for the collaborative blog *Designing Better Libraries* (http://dbl.lishost.org/blog/). More information from Bell about design for librarians can be found on his website (http://stevenbell .info/design).

DESIGN FOR EXPERIENCE: SERVICES FOR USERS WILL CHANGE YOUR LIBRARY

Library services are necessarily designed. Whether we're designing by intention or accident, our services go through "a process of originating and developing a plan for a product, structure, system, or component," which is Wikipedia's definition of the term *design*. In other words, every library service is at some point conceived, planned for, and implemented—whether we meant to do it methodically and through a formal design process or not. Design is not part of our training for library service, and unless we've acquired skills or experience elsewhere, or have a natural knack for it, library innovators, creative planners, and go-getters have become the accidental library designers.

But there's a design movement under way that asks designers to approach their work from the user perspective. *Experience* (or experiential) *design,* according to Wikipedia, is based on "the consideration of an individual's or group's needs, desires, beliefs, knowledge, skills, experiences, and perceptions." According to Marc Rettig, speaking at the Adaptive Path's User Experience Week 2005, "Designing for experience makes you change the questions [asked by the design process]. Experience design, or 'design for experience,' is a name for enlarging scope to consider patterns of life, goals, activity, context, repeated use, learning, sharing, emotion, and more . . . while applying The Design Process" (Rettig and Goel 2005). In this process, the context in which our users experience our services is key. It invites us to stay in tune with their desires, attentions, goals, and whatever else is happening around us. A few in our profession have already applied these concepts to libraries. Steven Bell, along with several others, contributes to the *Designing Better Libraries* blog. Librarian David Lee King published *Designing Digital Experiences* in 2008, and librarian Char Booth often writes about experience design on her blog *Infomational.* And though our first stop may seem to be designing library facilities and spaces, experience design can be used to develop any type of library service, space, or program.

The library building and physical space are critical to growing the social capital we explored in chapter 2. Ranganathan noted the importance of library places in 1931 when he instructed that "books are for use" and that they should be easily found and accessed regularly by all. Nancy Kranich called library places "the primary way" that libraries build social capital and called for continued access to "public space" or "commons" where "citizens can work together on personal and community problems" and "anchor" our neighborhoods with other public facilities (Kranich 2001). But what has changed, really, about the library as physical place since Ranganathan's appeal for better service? In many cases, I'm afraid, not much. Inspired by a talk given by Joe Janes, my mentor from the iSchool at the University of Washington, in my own talks I often show a photograph of the Library of Congress reference desk taken in 1906. Then I fast-forward to an image of the famous reading room in the academic library where I went to library school. Fast-forward again to my first job in a public library and you'll find a similar image (though not as gothic) of a reference desk lined with staff facing the entryway. The faces are a little friendlier than those of the librarians at the turn of the last century, but to my dismay we're all still sitting behind the same desks and in the same type of building.

Library spaces are central to the experiences of our users when they come inside the library facility. Designing for their experiences at the beginning of a facility design process can help identify what users want and need most out of their library experiences, making way for meeting rooms over reading rooms (or vice versa) or identifying where clear sight lines are necessary, where space for connecting and conversing is desirable, and where uninterrupted quiet space is required. Presenting collection areas with obvious headings that users understand (such as *magazines* instead of *periodicals*) considers our services from a user's perspective. Similarly, modular furniture and shelving units, methods of transferring light into space, and attention to distractions or unfiltered noise in multiuse spaces can give the library the presence and flexibility to respond to changing user needs over time. Dynamic, adaptable spaces allow for even the smallest of spaces to meet diverse needs and provide compelling experiences. Best of all, they stay relevant. David Adjaye's Idea Stores (with the tagline "Library, Learning, Information") in London have been called spaces that allow users to have "transformative educational experiences." Library architect William Brown calls this "design for lovability." *Library Journal* regularly hosts a Design Institute (East and West) for library practitioners beginning or early in the design process.

When designing a new facility is not necessary or practical, redesigning interior spaces may accomplish some of these same outcomes. In a 2007 study of sixty medium-sized to large public and academic libraries, John Sandy looked at the interior decorating projects libraries had completed over the preceding five years. Most often, both public and academic libraries chose to rearrange and upgrade furniture (including soft seating), repaint in stylish colors, upgrade light fixtures or window treatments, and acquire artwork (Sandy 2008). Beyond the library, regularly accessed commercial or public spaces make great extensions of the library space. Just outside Vancouver, British Columbia, a suburban branch library (Coquitlam Public) held its Books for BC Babies program in a local mall while the branch facility was being renovated. The program drew such an enormous turnout that Rhian Piprell, director of the library, told me it was like a light-bulb going on: *this is where we need to be.* The library now hosts an information kiosk in the library, staffed twice a month by library staff, and holds its Books for BC Babies program there permanently.

> Lovable libraries are not just places that people return to; they are places people return to with their friends and neighbors in tow. They make people feel elevated, comfortable, and social. Lovable libraries are more likely to be used, maintained, fought for, and preserved for generations. . . . Libraries that are loved have deep connections to the unique essence of their communities. They are woven into the fabric of residents' daily activities and resonate with the spirit, history, tradition, and culture of the neighborhood or the campus. Their locations are central to the paths people take on their daily treks. In the future, these treks may be shorter, more walkable, or more connected by mass transit and generally part of a more localized and collaborative way of life as fuel, food, and energy costs continue to rise.
>
> William M. Brown, "Future-Proof Design," 2008

Beyond our physical facilities and extended library spaces, libraries can and do create similar commons on their websites with "social" catalogs, blogs, online reader reviews, and hooks into Facebook, Twitter, YouTube, Flickr, or other popular networking sites where their users already "live" online. Programs also offer citizens the opportunity to gather around important issues and break down typical barriers between diverse users. The September Project began in 2001 in response to the need for American citizens to work through emotions and reactions to the then recent terrorist attacks in New York City. Beginning in 1996 with If All of Seattle Reads the Same Book, there are now more than fifty One Book, One Community programs across the United States, including The Big Read sponsored by the Library of Congress and the National Endowment for the Arts, as well as similar programs in Australia, Canada, and the United Kingdom. Wired for Youth at the Austin (Texas) Public Library provides computers, Internet access, and support for youth ages 8 to 17 from disadvantaged communities. The program focuses on learning how to use technology as a way of preparing for the future, not just the technology access itself. Coquitlam (British Columbia) Public Library allows users to "check out an expert," whereby library patrons can spend half-hour sessions with community members holding various perspectives or expertise ("check out a teenager" is my personal favorite). Janie Hermann at the Princeton (New Jersey) Public Library leverages patron expertise to deliver patron training on a number of different topics. Job training programs, information literacy projects, Books for Babies, English as a new language programs, community information centers, neighborhood directories, and voter or tax information can all be considered from the experiences of library users. All this requires a shift away from our understanding of the library as a resource that provides access to collections, materials, and other content for its own sake, and instead asks us to consider library services from the users' experiences with those materials and collections. In a discussion of why the library needs to present itself as transformational rather than informational, George Needham, former Michigan state librarian and current vice president of member services at OCLC, mentioned the example of patrons who ask for job interview or resume materials. "They don't want a book about resumes," he says; "they want a job." For an excellent resource on developing public library collections based on user needs, see Sharon Baker and Karen Wallace's *The Responsive Public Library* (2002).

TEENLINKS HOOKS TEENS INTO LIBRARY SERVICES
With Meg Canada

TeenLinks is the teen web portal for the Hennepin (Minnesota) County Library (HCL) website. Online since 1999, the site appears as the start page on 105 dedicated TeenLinks workstations in HCL's twenty-six libraries. The site's content is a community effort coordinated by a full-time Web Services/TeenLinks librarian. A team of six teen librarians serves as content selectors for ten different teen topical subject guides and thirteen homework help guides. Another group of ten librarians creates booklists covering teen interests, such as Body Angst, Manga, and Manga and Poetry for Teens. Two community members, a county public health communicator, and a university researcher in teen pregnancy act as advisory board members to the site.

The TeenLinks librarian mentors Teens Online, a volunteer teen advisory group. New teens apply to the group each year and represent all geographic areas that HCL serves. Teens Online determines its own goals each year and works as a whole or in subcommittees to meet them. Currently, thirteen teens gather monthly to write articles, develop quick polls, and select featured sites for TeenLinks. Over the years the group has contributed its own web pages, sponsored writing contests, and recorded book reviews as podcasts.

The site receives over 10,000 hits each week, and the users themselves have a part in TeenLinks. Teens can submit book reviews, enter contests, and use library resources. Book clubs and a summer book blog have also encouraged users to participate in the TeenLinks community. Like any full-service library, TeenLinks serves its community well. Teen events held at all twenty-six libraries are promoted, and registration is available on the website. Users can apply for library cards online, access virtual reference, and use readers' advisory tools. HCL's MySpace page mimics the TeenLinks design and brings visitors back to TeenLinks.

Since its inception TeenLinks has had two redesigns. The library's graphic designer, web administrator, TeenLinks librarian, and the aforementioned groups have all collaborated toward the vision of TeenLinks. Today's home page has more dynamically changing content, including new books, more photographs of local teens, and new weekly features such as the *News Flash* blog, quick poll, and events.

Meg Canada is a senior librarian in the Center for Innovation and Design at Hennepin County Library, Minneapolis. You can check out TeenLinks online at www.hclib.org/teens/.

The Carnegie Library of Pittsburgh, mentioned briefly in the preceding chapter, remains the best example that I've uncovered of a library deliberately seeking to reconsider its services, spaces, and collections based on the experiences of its users. Designers began with a simple photograph showing the interior of the library from a user's perspective upon entering. "This needs revolution, not evolution" became their design mantra. Initial scanning of the library's information environment identified three main areas: human resources (librarians, community), online resources (Internet, databases), and physical resources (books, facilities). Next, the designers articulated the library's goal to be a "preferred destination for knowledge, entertainment, and social interaction." Through a process of exploration, shadowing, and documentation, designers identified basic and substantive queries about each area. Next, they brainstormed, interviewed, and scrutinized the library through multiple sessions with staff and nonuser experiences with the library. Their research revealed key questions from the users' perspectives, such as "Is the library open or closed?" and "How do I start searching for a book?" Research also revealed inconsistencies in library instructions, service, signage, and spaces. In short, the library wasn't very "usable," and the experiences of library users boiled down to "I'm stupid" or "I'm confused."

MAYA (the design firm working on this project) developed a "complete customer experience cycle" that assumed that at "the end of every customer journey should be the beginning of a new one." A process of "rapid prototyping" showed multiple design options that would both meet user needs and match library capabilities. Library staff then prioritized their options based on the importance of the activity and the difficulty of implementing it, in an effort to spend their resources wisely. Their work culminated in three projects: an online experience (library website) that was consistent with the physical experience of being in the library, an intuitive catalog, and a physical space designed for dynamic information flow. They closed the loop by testing their designs with real users and refining those designs based on user experiences with them. Results, so far, indicate that overall and young adult circulation increased by leaps and bounds, in some cases by 187 percent.

Asking how the library can approach our services through the experiences of information seekers, and designing or in some cases redesigning our services to ensure that our users have good experiences with the library, which will prompt their return and continued engagement with us, not only will transform how our patrons view the library, it will transform the library itself.

PARTNER IS POWER

An interview with Cheryl Napsha on her library's work with a local nonprofit to meet needs for unique users

Tell us about yourself and your library.

I started in university libraries and quickly realized that public libraries were where the great social issues of our time will be realized. I'm interested in community building from all points of view—the physical, long-term community, and the idea that groups can come together for very short periods of time and create a community experience. We are a suburban library with no clear community identity, no physical or social center. My staff and I have focused on developing innovative services and programs to reach marginalized and vulnerable populations, and to enrich the lives of children of all ages. The staff have done an amazing job with the programs and services. . . . The demand is so great that only the budgetary constraints keep us from improving.

Is there something you've worked on that you'd call a successful community-building project?

In January 2006 we began working with the Homeless Children's Education Fund (HCEF), a nonprofit whose goal is to serve the eighteen homeless shelters in the county that focus on women and children (none of the shelters is in our service area). We began by issuing institutional cards to each shelter, then offering some basic programming on demand. That has grown as more shelters hear of the successes at other locations. The following spring the HCEF received a major grant to purchase materials for the learning centers in the shelters. Our library staff purchased $87,000 of books and DVDs and have since been building the libraries in each shelter. This program is limited only in that there is a finite amount of local money we can use to serve those outside our designated service area, but we hope to increase this through grants. In addition we plan to begin services to the county jail, which is developing a child-friendly waiting room and will need storytimes and programming.

Tell us how the project came together.

The HCEF project was serendipitous, resulting from information on the Allegheny County website stating that the largest growth in the homeless population was in children ages 2 to 10. We looked for some way to respond to that need.

What time, staff, and financial resources were required to get going?

We've diverted some staff time and funds from our general budget, and received a $3,000 stipend from HCEF for the collection development, but have expended close to $30,000 this year. Staff hours were just added to the general budget; supplies and materials were also taken from general funds. We approached our county federated library association for a grant to fund two part-time ongoing staff positions to develop regular weekly programming for the children and, eventually, for the mothers. Although the grant was not funded, the association staff are now seeking outside monies to continue the project.

At the time of this interview, Cheryl Napsha was the director of Bethel Park Public Library in Pennsylvania. She is now at the William P. Faust Public Library in Westland, Michigan. What hasn't changed is Cheryl's commitment to touch people's lives and connect them with public library services, wherever she lands.

CONVERGENCE AT YOUR LIBRARY: OPTIMIZE RESOURCES WITH LIBRARY PARTNERSHIPS

Institutions, organizations, and even individuals will find effective delivery of library services within their own resources difficult if not impossible to attain. Libraries should never go it alone. Inevitably, organizations striving to do their best with limited resources recognize their place in a larger system or framework—an ecological approach. Partnerships are key to staying vibrant and connected; they can save time, money, and even space. Williamsburg (Virginia) Regional Library went so far as to develop a formalized partnership process and to explicitly note that all organizations and sectors across its community are viable candidates for developing library partnerships (as long as the purpose of the partnership supports the library's mission!). Faced with a multitude of community, government, business, and personal connections we could foster, where should we start? One approach is to identify the critical customer needs that touch or concern multiple stakeholder groups. Finding common concerns and interests across sectors, institutions, and community members can help prioritize limited staff and financial resources toward the initiatives that will have the most (and most lasting) impact. Many libraries can easily identify the organizations and institutions where partnerships form naturally around shared services, purposes, facilities, or programs. Libraries are already revered for our partnerships with museums and other cultural institutions, schools, community centers, or community service providers, but let's take a look at an example of successful partnership that came out of mutual benefit and contributes both to sustainability and to community connections.

InfoZone is a fully operational, 3,000-square-foot branch library of the Indianapolis Marion County Public Library, housed entirely in the Children's Museum of Indianapolis. With its own collection, public access computers, in-branch laptop lending, and free wireless, the library has all the usual programs and services. It's the way these services are offered that's a bit of a departure from your average neighborhood library. Want to use the in-house laptops? You'll have to relinquish your shoes as collateral. Making use of the free Wi-Fi? Take a look at the library's actual web server, displayed and labeled in a plastic case! Want to learn more about the stuff you just saw in the museum? Check out the Discovery Kits (media/project bags filled with videos, books, and other educational materials) developed by library and museum staff, or browse the library collection via labels that match museum exhibits, instead of the standard Dewey Decimal numbers. Library and museum staff also worked together to create an image-driven database of museum collections, hosted by the library (www.imcpl.org/resources/digitallibrary/pictures.html). If Info-Zone's library services are a bit more fun, what other mutual benefits were identified during development of this partnership?

Before InfoZone opened in the Children's Museum in 2000, the museum attracted visitors from around the state but had trouble drawing children and residents from the local neighborhood. The library gave the museum a new way to reach out to locals and helped the museum provide a deeper educational experience to its visitors opting to take special kits or library materials related to the museum exhibits home with them. Similarly, the library was able to reach the residents and children in the local neighborhood (where branch services had been missing for almost twenty years!). Within months of its opening in the neighborhood, InfoZone became one of the highest-circulating branches in the system (it now serves more than 250,000 visitors per year) and became a new model for delivering children's services and resources across the system. Finally, both the museum and the library benefit from providing historical and cultural information to library and museum patrons visiting the online services, allowing them to serve not only local neighborhoods and the state of Indiana, but anyone with an Internet connection interested in the collections and information about them (www.imcpl.org/about/locations/infozone .html).

It may be easier to partner with organizations we identify immediately as natural companions because of shared purpose (schools, libraries, and museums all have education in mind, for example). But shared purpose and mutual benefit aren't mutually exclusive. Organizations that have very different missions, strategies, and cultures can still come together for planning, designing, and delivering greater community impact.

CHAPTER FIVE

Engage

Networked markets are beginning to self-organize faster than the companies that have traditionally served them. Thanks to the Web, markets are becoming better informed, smarter, and more demanding of qualities missing from most business organizations.
—The Cluetrain Manifesto

One thing I think many librarians have really struggled with is the idea of moving from being experts in their field to *collaborative* information mavens. Let me start a new mantra . . . *"people* formerly known as patrons." By opening this conversation we can begin to create the programs, products, and services *our customers will use.*
—Nancy Dowd, *The "M" Word: Marketing Libraries*

It MAY FEEL LIKE THE bulk of our community-building process is finished: we've listened, we've adjusted, we've changed. But the dialogue with our community that began with needs assessment can't simply come in one direction, inform our process, and stop there. Needs assessment and service design are just the conversation starters—a conversation that's two-way and ongoing. The next critical step our community-centric librarians revealed is to communicate directly and effectively with the community we're working with—about how the needs assessment and other strategic planning activities feed back to the library's mission, services, and vision for the future of our community.

At this point a portion of our community already knows a bit about what we've been up to. We've engaged them in evaluating community needs and in developing services to improve how we meet them. We have "a place at the table" with the city council, local schools and churches, and the chamber of commerce. More than likely, we already have good relationships with community members who were already engaged in the community and the thought leaders or stakeholders for communities we have yet to reach. But what can we do to carry this conversation forward and reach our whole community far and wide?

One answer lies in the discipline that many in Libraryland may still think of as sullied: marketing. I realize that mention of the term can provoke fervent cries against "business" practices and a call for libraries to retain their ethics and tradition of serving "the public good!" Conjuring notions of bait and switch, the hard-sell spin, and piles of profit, it's no wonder that some librarians shudder. Meanwhile, we're often accused of having few or poor skills in this area. Our long traditions of education, expertise, and public service are not often associated with customer needs or solutions. I believe that misunderstandings or misconceptions around both marketing and library practice may have led to an unnecessary resistance to their fusion, when they might fit together quite nicely. Are we really opposed to marketing? And are we really not skilled in this area? Let's take a closer look.

MISSING THE MARK: WHY DOES MARKETING HAVE SUCH A BAD REP?

Before we head into the basics of marketing and how these can be applied to our community-building endeavors, I'd like to explore what I see as some of the misconceptions or at least damaging beliefs about marketing. If we can begin to think of marketing outside its usual box, it may be easier to see how useful it might be to community building.

I believe that marketing is *unnecessarily* associated with private sector business practices, specifically the profit motive. Marketing is really very simple and doesn't require a financial bottom line. Marketing is about *finding and meeting customer needs.* Seems like a handy discipline, especially if we could boil it down to a few best practices that could work within any context. The problem is that a number of the concepts or frameworks for marketing strategy and implementation are geared toward private sector professionals who do have profit-making at stake, and this is unappealing to some librarians. But the fact that libraries have missions at stake does not make marketing any less useful or any less critical. I hope to show that even the most basic marketing principles, framed in terms of *our* bottom line (community building), can provide structure, reason, and clear steps toward better ongoing communication with the users we aim to serve.

Marketing is also sometimes associated with sales. The clear distinction between marketing and selling is that marketing aims to anticipate or find customer needs and fill them. Selling, on the other hand, starts with a product or service and aims it at a customer. (Not to put too fine a point on it, but—sound familiar?) The aim of marketing, the famous Peter Drucker once said, is to make selling unnecessary. (Not to put too fine a point on it, but—sound attractive?) By focusing on our patron's needs and showing clear efforts to meet them, effective marketing may make it unnecessary to talk about the laurels of the library in its own right, ever. Next, marketing should not be confused with advertising. The difference between marketing and advertising is that marketing, again, aims to anticipate or find customer needs and fill them. Advertising, on the other hand, is simply *one* method of communicating a specific message to a target set of customers. Advertising may or may not be the most appropriate method and should be considered one piece of the overall marketing plan.

As for not being any good at this stuff, what we may be missing is that library staff can be really good at building relationships and creating partnerships. We can be good at talking to people about their interests and needs, and helping them fill those needs. We can be good at connecting people with people and with meaningful content or useful tools. We can be good advocates for our patrons. And we're getting better at demonstrating the impact that our libraries make in their lives because of that advocacy. In this chapter, I aim to show that our accomplishments in these areas as a profession relate to the marketing basics I'll introduce. We're certainly not missing the skills and acumen for satisfying patron needs, but are perhaps simply missing the opportunity to dialogue proactively (and within a framework that pushes us forward) with patrons, partners, and other community stakeholders.

Finally, marketing is not just for marketers. Everyone in our organizations plays a part in anticipating and finding customer needs and in meeting those needs. Still, even with everyone pitching in, it's no small task. Marketing requires vision, education, and some structure or discipline for guidance. Once needs are clear and services designed, marketing should become the informal or formal responsibility of every person at every level of your organization, and your library's ability to form and build communities will thrive.

MARKETING BUILDS COMMUNITIES
An interview with Jill Stover

How did you become interested in marketing and libraries, and what does your blog offer libraries struggling to learn about and apply marketing principles to library practice?

I began studying library marketing while in library school. At the time, I was busy making a number of useful but labor-intensive online tutorials. I thought the tutorials could be a great help to students, but I wondered if they even knew about them. I realized that librarians do such incredible work but they need to do a better job of connecting their resources with students. Marketing is the way to do that. I started my blog, *Library Marketing—Thinking Outside the Book,* because I was learning a lot about marketing but wanted a vehicle for communicating those lessons. I believed it would also be a useful service for colleagues since there wasn't much writing on library marketing in the blogosphere at the time. I took the approach of linking business practice with library practice, not because businesses are better or because we should blindly mimic everything they do, but because the business literature is full of constructive models and methodologies that we should consider rather than ignore. Businesses have been strategically marketing for a long time, and we can learn from the business world just as we can learn from the education and psychology worlds, for example.

Do you think libraries struggle with marketing? Why?

Librarians struggle with marketing for any number of reasons, but three stand out: First, many feel a false sense of isolation from the world of commerce as nonprofit institutions. Second, there is a popular misconception that marketing only involves advertising and sales, which makes marketing merely an afterthought or, worse, irrelevant. And third, many libraries lack the financial means, time, leadership, and expertise to devote to marketing and so give up on it altogether.

What do you think is the most critical marketing concept/ principle that we could apply toward successful community building through libraries?

Communities are not large, homogeneous entities. Communities consist of groups of people with unique needs, wants, preferences, traditions, interests, etc. To identify and build communities, librarians need to find and learn as much as they can about those groups. For these reasons, market segmentation is a key marketing principle for librarians to grasp. Market segmentation involves breaking up large markets into smaller ones (segments) on the basis of shared characteristics. Librarians can segment target audiences using a number of different criteria such as demographics, attitudes, and lifestyles, to name a few.

What's the difference between libraries building community and integrating with our communities to make them stronger?

Librarians can approach marketing to communities in two ways: They can seek out existing communities, identify their unmet needs, and create services that fill those needs. Sometimes these communities are not highly visible, so careful market research and segmentation can help to uncover them. Librarians can also be the catalysts for forming library-centered communities. Hennepin County Public Library, for example, has done an excellent job of rallying teens around the library by gathering a group of them to create content for its TeenLinks website (www.hclib.org/teens/). In cases like this, the library itself is the binding force within the community.

What are some examples you've seen of how libraries can successfully segment or target their markets in order to better assess needs, develop services, and connect/communicate effectively with their communities?

I was really touched by a story I read about the Minneapolis Public Library and its outreach to new immigrant communities including Somalis, Hmong, and Latinos. (In this case, the segmentation variable was country of origin.) The immigrants have specialized needs, and so the library restructured its services to accommodate them. The library now offers literacy training, a multilingual website, and language-learning tools. Its bookmobile also appears at community events. Staff even wear handcrafted pouches created by Hmong immigrants as a welcoming gesture. This is a terrific example of a library that strategically sought out communities it could best serve and aligned its services, and even its attitude, accordingly. Done right, marketing creates real value for people and can even be life-changing for community members.

Jill Stover is the undergraduate services librarian for the James Branch Cabell Library, Virginia Commonwealth University, where she creates and promotes library services for undergraduates. You can find her online at http://librarymarketing.blogspot.com.

MARKETING BASICS: THE FOUR PS, AND THEN SOME

Let's reiterate: marketing is not about libraries, nor is it about library services. It's about our community. It's about their needs. In the simplest of terms, marketing "anticipates and meets customer demand" (Hart 1999, 7). When we jump down into the details, it may be helpful to come back to this mantra: our aim is to anticipate and meet customer needs. As I said, library staff are already pretty good at some of this stuff. It's just a matter of pulling all that skill into a process that can help keep us on track and moving forward.

First coined by Jerome McCarthy in 1960, the four Ps represent the essential elements of any marketing strategy from a management perspective. More recently, R. Lauterborn (1990) updated these elements to the four Cs to remind us that marketing should be approached from the customer as well as the management perspective. I've combined these approaches in the following review.

Product > Customer Solution. What are our customers' needs? How will the library meet customer needs? Launching into a marketing strategy for the library as the product or service designed to meet those needs may overwhelm. Begin instead with a small service or opportunity. The service might be general and broad, such as adult reference, or it might be specific and focused, like online databases. Make a list of every feature of the product or service *as it relates to the needs of the target group you identified.* Coming from a long tradition—as we do in libraries—of service, learning and knowledge stewardship values, and social good, it can be very helpful to articulate exactly how the product or service relates to patron needs. If it doesn't, perhaps that's one opportunity for service improvement, redefinition, or even abandonment.

Price > Cost. What will it cost your target customers to access the library's product or service? Take a deep breath here, and don't assume that everything in your library is free. The library has charged monetary fees for several things for a very long time. Keeping books for extended periods (beyond their due date) is a fee-based service. Photocopying and printing are often fee-based, as is parking or additional research in many libraries. And while monetary cost may be our first consideration, the library service or solution may require that our customers give up something else of value: time, effort, convenience, or anonymity, for example. Perhaps we require that patrons overcome social embarrassment or stigma in order to access the library collections, programs, or services. So answer simply—is your service free or fee-based? If there is no financial cost to patrons, what are their other costs to obtain the service?

Place > Convenience. Where will the product or service be delivered to best meet customer needs? Does delivery take place in the library building? At the desk? On the phone? Through the bookmobile? At the mall? Through a kiosk? At the county fair? At a company picnic? On the website? On Facebook? At some other point of need? Describe every possible place your service will be rendered, and prioritize these locations according to how well the placement responds to your target audience, their needs, and where they are. Consider the habits and preferences of your audience, as well as any knowledge you may have of their current use of and/or satisfaction with various distribution channels already in place at your library.

Promotion > Communication. How will you let your audience know about your product or service? Promotion describes the messages you'll use to describe customer needs and how your service aims to meet those needs. Advertising is one form of promotion. Branding, naming, public relations, word-of-mouth, buzz, direct messaging, and user stories are all examples, and we'll talk about these in more detail.

When pulled together, the Ps and Cs represent a basic marketing mix. If you want to dig deeper into the key principles and resources for effective marketing, you'll find references to the four Ps, or the five Ps, or the seven Ps, or the nine Ps, and so on. Ultimately, you'll find that different marketing resources and experts may use different terms to describe the concepts listed earlier. They may add concepts such as *people, partners, process, philosophy,* or even *purse strings.* All these can add to your marketing strategy as long as you remember your most basic elements and continue to constantly evaluate, add, delete, and improve to find a strategy that works for your community and your library. In the following section, I'll uncover a few elements that I believe come into play for libraries. For consideration of how the four Ps apply to libraries and information science, see the first chapter of Irene Owens's *Strategic Marketing in Library and Information Science: A Selected Review of Related Literature* (2002).

PUTTING PATRONS ON THE MAP
With Molly Rodgers

Wayne County, Pennsylvania, is a rural county along the northern Delaware River, but during the summer months the local library looks and sounds more like a branch of the United Nations, with dozens of languages being spoken and alphabets other than English on the computer screens. The county has a lot of summer camps, and young people come from all over the world to work as camp counselors. With rivers, lakes, and state forests, the area also attracts summer visitors. Hundreds of people use the library's public access computers to stay in touch with family and friends, to contact travel agencies and airlines, and to search for information about the local area and other places they plan to visit.

In the summer of 2004, we put up a world map in our public access computer room and asked all the patrons using a computer to put a dot on the map to show their home country, as well as write down the name of their hometown on a legal pad. After the summer was over, we used the map and the list of place names in presentations to local service clubs and to public officials. The map was an effective way to show how people from all over the world depend on the computers at public libraries, and we shared some of the stories of how our staff and our services made visitors feel welcome. The presentations were especially effective with service groups that have international missions such as Rotary Clubs. Most people had no idea of the influx of computer users we have during the summer! The local Rotarians decided to apply for a matching grant to purchase a laptop computer for us with a wireless Internet connection. This grant allowed us to expand the number of computer stations we can offer and will support other sources of funding to increase our wireless capacity.

In addition to the international character of summer visitors and campers who come to our libraries, we now see an increasing number of people living and working in Wayne County who have come from other countries. Library computers are vital to these new residents as they search for jobs, type resumes, take courses in English as a new language, and practice citizenship and TOEFL (Test of English as a Foreign Language) tests. We recently invited our three county commissioners to a library that had received new computers this year through the Gates Opportunity Grant, to thank them for providing matching funds. One of the library patrons who spoke about the importance of public access computers in his own experience is from Colombia. Showing—and telling—our community about the library's global reach and local outcomes has made a huge difference.

Molly Rodgers is director of the Wayne County Public Library in rural Pennsylvania and administrator of the Wayne Library Authority, a system of seven libraries in the county. Her career goal is to break down old stereotypes and change local perceptions about libraries and librarians. Her library is online at www.waynelibraries.org.

MARKETING STRATEGIES FOR SOCIAL GOOD: LIBRARY USERS, NOT THE LIBRARY

In the early 1970s, P. Kotler and G. Zaltman (1971) noticed that marketing ideas, processes, and practices were being used to influence target audiences toward actions for the benefit of themselves, their groups, or society as a whole. The authors coined the term *social marketing* (as distinct from *consumer marketing* as outlined earlier), and the discipline developed, primarily through health-behavior-related ventures, through the last part of the twentieth century. Marketing consultant Nedra Weinreich calls social marketing "an approach that benefits the people who are adopting the behaviors or society as a whole, rather than the organization doing the marketing" (www.squidoo.com/socialmarketing/). More recently, the U.K.'s National Social Marketing Center (2000) developed a working definition of social marketing as "the systematic application of marketing concepts and techniques, to achieve specific behavioural goals, to achieve a social or public good." According to the center, social marketing has three main elements:

- It aims to achieve a particular "social good" (rather than commercial benefit) with specific behavioral goals clearly identified and targeted.
- It is a systematic process phased to address short-, medium-, and long-term issues.
- It utilizes a range of marketing techniques and approaches (a marketing mix).

Social marketing principles can help libraries move the discipline of traditional consumer marketing into a context of libraries building communities. In addition to pulling the four Ps through a mission-based outlook, social marketing can bring in several factors that are typical of most social enterprises. Following are the additional factors I believe to be most critical to the library's marketing mix.

People. As discussed in chapter 4, it's essential to identify who the library intends to serve and what their needs are. For librarians building community, inclusion is key. Start with the broadest definition of your community, whether that is a school, a specific organization, a city, a county, or a state. While broad definitions of community remind us to serve our whole community, launching into a library marketing strategy for "our community" can be a bit overwhelming and difficult to characterize, keeping us from moving forward at all. So our next step is to identify the audiences that make up the community we serve, or to break up the larger community into smaller market segments. To do this, make a list of every group of customers the library serves, no matter how small. Segmenting your community into smaller groups starts with a list of potential shared characteristics for group members, such as age, location, frequency of use, day/time of use, ability/willingness to pay, employment status or role, subject interest, format preferences, specific needs or problems, or even factors that ensure patron success in terms of needs met. And of course, don't forget the segments of our communities that are not already aware of or using the library.

Segmenting your total market can help you focus on customer needs and problems, instead of the management issues related to consumer marketing, and is especially important for marketers. Because of our history, traditional services, and frequent access to some of our community members, library staff can get caught up in assumptions about who customers are and about their needs and desires. Stepping back to identify all possible customers, and proposing needs from their perspective, can help us avoid assumptions, especially where those assumptions are no longer serving the customers we aim to serve. Market segmentation can also help us develop marketing plans that allocate resources and effort across the entire community based on highest need, largest number served, and other factors. Finally, market segmentation can help us develop marketing messages that really speak to the target audiences. Unless books are the solution for your whole community, and you're already reaching every individual with your current collection, highlighting specific solutions that benefit particular members of your community in very specific ways—ones that are meaningful to *them*—can position the library as a central force.

Once target audiences are identified and characterized, take one or a few groups and try to prioritize them based on their needs or on your area of service within the library. Choose just one audience and approach your first marketing strategy for that group. You can later expand your strategy to include additional target audiences. Now that you've got your people, or target audience, identified, go back to your needs assessment findings and make a list of the needs that are specific to this group. This step is the key to the product or service your library is offering. Terry Kendrick's *Strategic Marketing Plans That Really Work: A Toolkit for Public Libraries* (2006) is a useful overall marketing resource, with a chapter dedicated to library market segmentation and another to setting priorities.

Partners. Who are the key players in offering your service? Though the library is certainly poised for building strong communities, surely no single organization has the ability to build community all by itself! Partnering with other organizations distributes the talents and skills of multiple groups across your project and distributes responsibility and sustainability across organizations. Make a list of all the people required to make your product or service as successful as it can be. Partnerships can range from informal cooperation based on shared interest to full-scale collaboration based on formal relationships and shared missions. Partners may include key library staff, volunteers, other organizations, thought leaders, decision makers, advisors, or even customer groups (such as evangelists or early adopters). Thinking initially about all the possible partners who may influence the success of your service may give you a leg up when it comes to evaluating the effectiveness or quality of the service for meeting the needs you've identified.

Funding. Library service funding is critical to our overall marketing mix. If the service is offered at no monetary cost to patrons, make a note of how the service is funded (we'll get back to this in a moment) and brainstorm any other possible costs for your audience. If the service is fee-based, provide some explanation about how the price was identified. Also indicate whether the price is meant to simply cover costs to break even or if some profit is meant to be acquired with the price you've identified. Finally, identify how the service or product will be funded, if not directly by the customer.

Value Proposition. A value proposition is your publicly directed "elevator pitch" that describes how your service will meet the needs of your target audience. The value proposition is a one- to two-sentence description of why the customer wants the library service, written in language that the customer understands and responds to. The value proposition should focus on the benefits to the customer, not the features of the service.

Process. Marketing strategies are very similar to the processes for building community outlined in this book. If you weave marketing plans into your overall strategic planning, service design and delivery, and even evaluation efforts, your marketing efforts will also be an iterative process of assess, design, engage, iterate, and sustain.

Now that we have the basic elements down, and a framework for using them outside traditional consumer marketing models, it may be easier to pull them together into a marketing strategy that makes sense for libraries building community. One place to start is to identify all your Ps on the accompanying marketing strategy worksheet. This process will encourage clear, succinct descriptions, and you'll begin to see more clearly how all the elements fit together *and* how they each relate to our most basic tenet: anticipating and aiming to meet our customers' needs.

MARKETING STRATEGY WORKSHEET

...

Use this worksheet to organize your thoughts on marketing your library, specific collections, or special projects.

MARKETING STRATEGY FOR [*insert product or service*]:

_____

_____

PEOPLE. List the target audiences for the product or service, broken down into market segments and with brief descriptions.

_____

_____

PROBLEMS. List the needs of your audience, in relative order of importance.

_____

_____

PRODUCT. List the features of your product or service, in direct relationship to the needs.

_____

_____

PRICE. Identify the price or cost (to target audience members) for accessing the product or service.

_____

_____

PLACE. List the channels by which you'll distribute the product or service, in order of convenience to the target audience.

_____

_____

PROMOTION. List ways you'll let your target audience know about the product or service.

_____

_____

VALUE PROPOSITION. Write a one- to two-sentence description of why the customer wants the product or service, using language that your customer understands. Focus on benefits to the customer, not features of the product or service.

_____

_____

PARTNERS. List those you plan to partner with to ensure product/ service success and adoption.

_____

_____

FUNDING. Describe where the funding comes from, how long you'll have access to it, and how the product or service will be sustained in the long term.

_____

_____

TRENDS TOWARD ENGAGEMENT: USER PARTICIPATION DRIVES AWARENESS AND LOYALTY

Granted, there are good reasons some of us associate marketing with pushing products on people who don't want them. For the last part of the twentieth century, our consumer experience involved big companies partnering with bigger media to create complete and utter bombardment by marketing messages. Many of the marketing principles described earlier are traditional, brand-centric, message-controlled, marketing concepts. It's helpful to have these marketing principles in our tool kit. They can help tighten messages and make sure we have a sound plan in place. But I'd be remiss to cover only these marketing principles, because marketing is changing, and it's all about participation.

Markets didn't used to care much about humans. It was all about products, consumers, and transactions. You might even say that some librarians haven't cared much about humans. It was all about services, collections, and circulation. Enter social media, enter social companies, enter social products, enter social. "If the last ten years have caused disruption in your business, the next ten years will cause much more so," begins the 2005 business reference *Communities Dominate Brands: Business and Marketing Challenges for the Twenty-first Century.* "Not driven by a controlled introduction of new technologies, but by an uncontrolled adoption of new, radical, unpredictable and even 'unfair' methods by an emerging new element in consumption—*the digitally empowered community*" (Ahonen and Moore 2005, 1). Beginning with the Internet, as in the open source software movement, consumers started to get together online and create useful products for themselves. Beginning with Web 2.0 (where consumers aren't your typical techie types anymore and technology is almost completely out of our way), anyone with an interest and an Internet connection can get together with a like-minded person online and create products for themselves.

In this environment, traditional controlled-message marketing just doesn't work. Consumers are smarter and savvier and have more power and influence over themselves and their consumer decisions. "We're living in the most cluttered marketplace in history," says Seth Godin, a new media marketing consultant, in *Flipping the Funnel.* "Whether you are curing cancer, encouraging faith or educating people in need, people are better at ignoring you than ever before" (2006, 3). Inspired by websites like the Cluetrain Manifesto (www.cluetrain.com), participatory, community-oriented, engagement, or open source marketing takes advantage of the new media environment by actively engaging consumers in needs assessment, product development, and service delivery, and even the messaging about these processes.

The Texas A&M University Libraries took a novel approach to developing a marketing campaign to advertise the availability of 30,000 NetLibrary books. Teaming with its American Advertising Federation student chapter, the library was able to deliver a "creative, student-focused advertising campaign" that resulted in the creation of "200 new user accounts and 3,800 e-book circulations within the first two weeks" (McGeachin and Ramirez 2005, 139). Whether you call it participatory or open source, new media marketing is based in conversation: between consumers, between consumers and organizations, and between organizations. As with assessment and planning, engaging community members in conversation with library staff, with other organizations, and with each other may mean that we lose absolute authority over the process, but the outcomes will be informal, honest, *human* conversations that lead to lasting *relationships* with the communities we aim to serve. As these trends continue to emerge, library staff experimenting with these new tools discover more and more frequently that they're on the same playing field with their users. The same tools we use to communicate and connect with one another as professionals sit alongside the interactions we're having with users. Together, we learn and engage in a way that no longer values the librarian's expertise over the user's.

UN-MARKETING
An interview with Michael Porter

Tell us about your library staff workshop on "un-marketing."

Helene Blowers and I created this workshop together. Looking back over the years we'd spent working in libraries, we realized that we were working on similar things: ways to help people tell their personal stories of "how the library is important to me and my community." The workshop includes a collection of meaning-ful library stories, success stories of community and technology engagement, and a brainstorming session with participants that we hope is both inspiring and motivating.

Why did you create the workshop?

We're interested in both traditional communication channels and using emerging technologies to tell library stories. We were also trying to find ways to inspire, collect, and share local stories of people successfully engaging with library content, services, and community. Finally, we were actively looking for ways to share stories of how technology and library services, both traditional and innovative, were shaping and nurturing communities across the world.

What happened when you did your first workshop?

We both got really excited about the powerful stories of commu-nity connection and inspiration and sharing out there that other folks were creating. Libraries and library staff all over the world are doing *amazing* things that use the voices of their patrons and supporters to encourage use and support of libraries. There was no way we could know about the things going on out there in Libraryland and not try to get the word out!

What "counts" as un-marketing?

Un-marketing is a way of empowering people to share their library-related success stories. It is a way to praise citizenry and highlight the value of library services. It takes the power of new technology and puts it together with local talent, work, and care to create a package that makes the whole greater than the sum of its parts. It is the pictures of the summer reading program events at the library, posted to Flickr, that warm the hearts of the folks at the retirement community. Un-marketing is the guest blog post from the local business owner who tells the com-munity that she wouldn't have succeeded without the resources the library offers. Un-marketing is the library MySpace or Flickr page that has hundreds of "friends" listed, most of whom are from within a twenty-mile radius. Most of all, un-marketing is a way to share, connect, create, grow, and expand the story and value of the library as a vibrant and valuable community institution.

Michael Porter is a librarian, author, presenter, and PEZ collector. His un-marketing workshop with Helene Blowers is available through Information Today's pre-conference workshops, and you can follow his blog at www.libraryman.com.

A CONNECTED COMMUNITY: WHAT'S YOUR LIBRARY'S BRAND?

The library's brand is its most important marketing message. Though we have yet to discuss it, even traditional branding is, very simply, (1) identifying who you speak to, (2) knowing what you have to say, and (3) making a real connection, or "meaning it" when you deliver the message (Girvin Strategic Branding and Design 2002). Again, it's all stuff librarians are already good at. Our approach to marketing takes these basic concepts and pulls them into practice that keeps the community at the forefront of our plans, strategies, and activities. Many libraries are struggling to survive, never mind thrive, in this rapidly changing environment. Instead of building our brand around our collections and services, we should be building it around the people we aim to serve.

According to OCLC's *Perceptions of Libraries and Information Resources* report (De Rosa 2005), "the Library brand is dominant in one category—books." Books are our brand. Instead, the word *library* needs to speak to our communities. Libraries need to reflect back to our users our collective interests and needs. Our programs and services are mirrors to our patrons and partners. As they change, we change. Our messages, delivered consistently and successfully, will support and instill the value of our community. In essence, our community members must see themselves in our brand, and they must be able to articulate, in two or three sentences, how "the library is about *us*" and how "my library is about *me.*" The key here is that the goal of our brand is to create compelling *relationships* with our users. If we reflect our community members, the brand will remain meaningful and human. So, how do we get there? Developing a library brand is one component of the overall marketing strategy. There are myriad new marketing resources to get you started. Once you've had a chance to dig a little deeper, try the following five steps (adapted from *The Community Networking Handbook* [Bajjaly 1999]) for creating a marketing plan for your library, keeping in mind traditional marketing strategies as well as new ways of engaging communities through conversation for more participatory marketing practices.

1. Set Goals

What do you hope to accomplish with your marketing efforts? Goals can be related to your image (for example, actively raise awareness about the library or a new library service) or to the way the library is perceived (for example, actively change perceptions about the library's main service from book borrowing to public access computing). Goals can also be related to individual accomplishments or behaviors (for example, number of website or library visits). As with defining your audience, setting goals can be tricky. Thinking broadly is encouraged *to the point that it's useful.* Thinking too broadly can overwhelm and keep you from moving forward. Start with a smaller, specific marketing project, set reasonable goals that you're able to track, and move on to your next step.

2. Conduct an Audit

How much is your organization already doing to accomplish goals? Who's already doing the work? What resources are available for your marketing effort? This is where the four Ps (and Cs) come in. Brainstorming every product–customer solution, price–cost, place–convenience, and promotion–communication will give you a good idea about where your library is starting in the process.

3. Position the Library

What is it that your library does that others do not? In honestly and succinctly articulating the differentiators between your library and other organizations, you establish your niche and the justification for the library or your services to your patrons, to staff, to decision makers, and to other stakeholders. By asking your customers why they come to the library, you may identify new ways to talk about the library or your services. This is the beginning of your local library brand.

4. Develop a Plan

How does each of the Ps or Cs align with marketing goals? What needs to be done? Who will do it? When will it be done? What are the milestones? Where will the time, staff, or funding come from? Similar to the marketing mix worksheet, a cohesive marketing plan will help keep you focused on key audiences and messages, tactics for engaging them, and available resources.

5. Create a Campaign

How will you get the word out? This step is where marketing relates to advertising and other promotions, and we turn all our attention to the promotion aspect of the marketing mix. Promotion includes both the *message (vehicle)* and the *tactic (avenue)*. An effective message "motivates your audience to take a specific action (as defined in your original goals) and promises a desirable benefit if they do. Your promotional message should specifically ask your audience to take a next step" (Bajjaly 1999, 122). Avenues for getting messages out can be anything from traditional ad placements to extremely targeted messaging via RSS. Better yet, help your patrons tell each other how library services, collections, or connections are most useful.

Staying connected with library professionals who value and regularly experiment with marketing can be a great source of inspiration and support as you approach your own marketing strategies or try experimenting with new messages and tactics (see the text box "Marketing Tactics"). Nancy Dowd's *The "M" Word—Marketing Libraries* and Brian Mathews's *The Ubiquitous Librarian* are useful marketing blogs specific to library services that provide excellent ongoing resources in addition to the publications mentioned in this chapter.

Whether we call it marketing or advocacy, we need to get better at what marketing and customer-relationship gurus have known for years: the library needs to create and build the story of our relationship with the community we work with. If we're willing to take a step back from common misconceptions about consumer-based marketing and shift our

MARKETING TACTICS

Here's a nice mix of old and new marketing tactics to consider when creating your next marketing campaign. Low- or no-cost tactics are in bold; you can try these out with little staff or financial resources. See if they work for your library.

advertising	**letters to the editor**
annual reports	**networking**
attitude	news conferences
audio (podcasting)	newsletters
billboards	posters
blogs	presentations
brand	**press releases**
brochures	publications
buzz	public service announce-
connect and converse with	ments
patrons	RSS
direct mail	sales
editorials	**social networking**
emerging technologies of any	specialty items; swag
kind	talk shows, public television
endorsements	telethon/telemarketing
events	text messaging/mobile
feature stories	technologies
flyers	video (videocasting)
get out from behind the desk	wikis
get out of the library	**word of mouth**

thinking to social or mission-based marketing, it's a bit easier to see how marketing might be useful, if not critical, to the library's community-building efforts. With the suggestion that we turn our focus away from talking about the library and toward talking about the community, we see a strong synergy between marketing practice and community-building principles. Marketing can also provide a structure or framework for communicating both efficiently (saying it right) and effectively (saying the right things), critical for staying connected in a culture of accountability to our public, our staff, and our funders. With even the slightest bit of strategy and careful planning, a marketing venture can place us in strong connection with our target audiences, produce fuller cooperation with partners, and create deeper support from decision makers and all our stakeholders. Most important, it engages us in genuine and dynamic interactions with our community members, perhaps opening the possibility of hosting them as vested, valued partners in everything the library does.

CHAPTER SIX

Iterate

Project met goals. Participants were satisfied. The library made some money.

· · ·

I believe that touching the lives of marginalized populations just can't be measured in any true way.

· · ·

As far as measurement, I ask people in the community how we are doing. That's it.

· · ·

Participants were very happy, and anxious to do it again and again!

· · ·

Participation was higher than we'd anticipated by quite a bit. Evaluations were positive. Requests for repeat have been many.

—Various respondents in answer to our survey question, "Tell us about impacts and outcomes. Did the project meet its goals? How was this measured?"

EVALUATION. MEASUREMENT. DATA. IMPACT. With time, staff, and financial resources already scarce and plenty else to do, it is difficult for most of us to imagine covering all (and overall) library services with a comprehensive evaluation plan. Instead of going with data, we go with our guts. Sometimes we're right on with our intuitive understanding of how well our library is connected to and impacting our communities, but imagine showing up to your library's next trustee, city council, or board meeting with the statements at the beginning of this chapter bulleted on a PowerPoint: not very much impact, not necessarily efficient. Yes, in Libraryland, we have work to do in this area.

Evaluation can be challenging from many angles. At the very least, it requires commitment from library leaders and practitioners—we have to understand evaluation and believe in its importance. Even then, evaluation can be overwhelming, especially without orientation, training, or special interest in the discipline. There's a lot to take in on the topic and even a review of the literature can be difficult. Evaluation can also be expensive. A long-term and iterative practice, it requires dedicated and ongoing investments in training, planning, collecting, analyzing, and communicating what we've learned. Finally, evaluation is multifaceted, concerned with not only what we do but also whether it matters. Uncovering the part about whether library services matter to individuals can be as easy as talking to patrons whose accomplishments can be directly related to library experiences. But when it comes to the difference we make to families, organizations, and our communities as a whole, evaluation becomes much more complicated.

Comprehensive evaluation, however powerful, requires new approaches and a long-term, community-centered outlook that many library staff may feel they just can't afford. Whether it's staff time, money, too much to make sense of, or too much else to do, our profession is well known for forgoing formal evaluation programs for more intuitive management and communication styles. Our library is good. We make a difference. We change lives. We do our best with what we have. Our community values and trusts our library. Sound familiar? To some extent, our answer to these challenges has been to drown out our need for a more rigorous evaluation process with well-intentioned, but still "faith-based," convictions and appeals.

Whatever the challenge, and wherever we are in our response to those challenges, I believe it's possible to boil down the essentials of evaluation into something that libraries of any size or type can take to (and from) our library practice. In simple terms, evaluation should be used to tell us where we have been, where we are, and where we're headed in relation to the community we're serving. The measures we choose and analyze should also guide our decisions and help us improve our process and service as we plan for the future. This chapter will outline a brief history of planning and evaluation in libraries that will help set the context for creating your own evaluation plans, uncover the basics of an evaluation process, explain how to use these basics to enhance your overall community building approach, and point you to current resources in this area. At the end of this chapter you'll have the information and tools you'll need to outline a basic evaluation program; you can then turn to your library's initiatives and sketch out your plans for approaching evaluation in your library.

RETURN ON INVESTMENT: NEW RESEARCH FOCUSES ON DEMONSTRATING IMPACT

According to James Matarazzo and Lawrence Prusak, a survey of senior managers in large U.S. corporations revealed that "more than 60 percent could not give a specific value of the library in their organization" (Matthews 2002, xiv). In response, many libraries and library service organizations are working to calculate and articulate their return on investment (ROI) to their stakeholders. Joseph Matthews and others have explored library ROI more fully and provided excellent resources or examples for developing your own ROI model. Following are a few examples of some recent ROI studies in different types of libraries.

Taxpayer Return on Investment in Florida Public Libraries (Griffiths 2004). This study summarizes research conducted for the State Library and Archives of Florida in 2003 and 2004 by investigators from the University of North Carolina at Chapel Hill, the University of Pittsburgh, and Florida State University. The study used several approaches to considering returns on public library availability and use and found that all showed returns exceeding investment. For example, for every $6,448 in public funds spent on Florida's public libraries, one job was created. Every dollar of public support spent on Florida's public libraries produced an increase of $9.08 in gross regional product and an increase of $12.66 in total state wages.

Southwestern Ohio's Return from Investment in Public Libraries (Levin, Driscoll, and Fleeter 2006). Researchers showed that nine public library systems in southwestern Ohio created an annual economic impact of nearly four times the amount invested in their operations. According to the study, for every dollar expended on library operations, the public received about $2.56 in directly quantifiable benefits.

The Seattle Public Library Central Library: Economic Benefits Assessment (Berk and Associates 2005). Research revealed that the Seattle Public Library's new central building, featuring the work of OMA's Rem Koolhaus, produced an increase in library visits of 300 percent in the first year after opening. Revenues in the surrounding district went up by 16 percent, library circulation went up by 50 percent, and public access computer use more than quadrupled.

Making Cities Stronger: Public Library Contributions to Local Economic Development (Urban Libraries Council 2007). This study was commissioned by the Urban Libraries Council, funded by the Bill and Melinda Gates Foundation and the Geraldine R. Dodge Foundation, and released in January 2007. The research found that public libraries build a community's capacity for economic activity and resiliency. Specifically, early-literacy services, library employment and career resources, small-business programs, and public library buildings were all found to contribute to economic and social success within the libraries' communities.

FROM FAITH TO FACT TO IMPACTS: A VERY SHORT HISTORY OF EVALUATION IN LIBRARIES

Most librarians believe that libraries are good. Our facilities, collections, and services have been associated with the goodwill of our customers, benefactors, and the public since the late nineteenth and early twentieth centuries, when libraries were already well established by public and private support. We also know, or at least believe, that the library supports the public good—that is, the improvement of targeted individuals, institutions, and their communities. But how do we *know* libraries are good for individuals or their communities? And what difference does it make? Articulating library "goodness" has been on a path from faith ("we just know") to fact ("here's how we know") to impact ("here's why it matters") over the course of the last century, and it winds through library statistics, standards, planning models, and new pressures on the social sector (Orr 1973; Dees, Economy, and Emerson 2001; McCook 2004). Sure to evolve over the coming century, our current evaluation efforts benefit from the progress our profession has made in each of these areas.

Between the 1930s and the 1950s, library associations developed library service standards comprising basic statistics and checklists that libraries could use to develop models for minimum and improved services. This work culminated in the 1956 publication of *Public Library Service: A Guide to Evaluation, with Minimum Standards* (ALA 1956). Just as library service was focused internally on maintaining, organizing, and providing (sometimes limited) access to collections and materials, library evaluation was internally focused on our own resources and processes. Many state library agencies continue standards work today, and a number of state-specific minimum library standards are updated and published regularly as part of a broader case for library sustainability.[1]

By the late 1960s, libraries moved to gathering and reporting a broader range of descriptive statistics, and the Public Library Association (PLA) initiated a planning process that helped libraries develop their own goals to meet community needs. As library services responded to a national call for meeting local community needs, library evaluation methods followed suit. In 1980, PLA published manuals for local planning: *A Planning Process for Public Libraries* and a companion manual, *Output Measures for Public Libraries.* For public libraries, early work culminated in the 1987 publication of *Planning and Role Setting for Public Libraries: A Manual of Options and Procedures.* The book identified eight roles for public libraries, ranging from supporting community activities and information to providing popular materials and research centers. By 1995, public libraries had successfully moved from standards to planning, and investigators observed, in hindsight, that local innovations can be facilitated by associations and other library service agencies. In the private sector, special libraries were also struggling with how to demonstrate and articulate value. A 1990 study of senior managers in large U.S. corporations indicated that more than half could not specifically identify the value that their own libraries brought to their organization (Matarazzo and Prusak 1990). Throughout the 1990s the Special Libraries Association (SLA) published a number of works addressing the value of special libraries (SLA 1993–2000).

The 1990s and the turn of the twenty-first century ushered in an increased focus on library service relationships to community needs, along with a new focus on bottom line performance toward meeting those needs. Planning methods focused on building the capacity for library management to plan for, deliver, and articulate "library excellence." In the United States, this movement was initiated by two major pressures on the social sector: first, in the public sector, a move by the federal government in 1993 to formalize and require documented accountability for efficiency to the public; and second, in the private sector, new concepts in business around "social enterprise" and a move to commercialize some formerly philanthropic or nonprofit operations.

The Government Performance Results Act of 1993 "seeks to shift the focus of government decision making and accountability away from a preoccupation with the activities that are undertaken . . . to a focus on the results of those activities" (www.whitehouse.gov/omb/mgmt-gpra/ gplaw2m.html). Under the act, agencies are required to develop multiyear strategic plans, annual performance plans, and annual reports. Because many libraries are affiliated with city, county, state, or other government entities and are primarily supported by public funding, it was only a matter of time before the act would impact library practice. Meanwhile, nongovernment benefactors, funders, and supporters of libraries are increasingly interested in their investments in libraries. They want to know if our spaces, buildings, programs, services, and projects are achieving desired results. More recently, in their book *How Libraries and Librarians Help* (2005), Joan Durrance, Karen Fisher, and Marian Hinton identify an "urgent need to tell the library story more effectively." Economic downturns, swings of the political pendulum, the clear need for vital services like police and emergency services—all call into question the services of the library, especially if we've not taken care to match those services with community needs or not stayed in touch with our community about how we're meeting their needs.

Concurrently, changes were taking place in the U.S. private sector, prompted primarily by business schools. In 2001 Harvard Business School professor J. Gregory Dees published *Enterprising Nonprofits,* which identified the forces stimulating commercialization of the social sector. Dees identified the similarities and differences between for-profit and not-for-profit projects and called for those in the social sector to approach their objectives in much the same way that commercial enterprises do: by adding value to the resources that they acquire and process, but to do so with care. Dees identified three major differences between social and commercial enterprises: (1) the bottom line, (2) the price, and (3) methods for obtaining resources. Dees suggests that social enterprises operate toward a customized bottom line—that of positive social outcome, instead of commercial profit. Second, social enterprise products and services are often free or offered at less than their actual cost. Social enterprises, however, are dependent on financial or other contributions to stay in operation. In spite of these differences, Dees maintains, social and commercial sectors should be conceptually operating in the same way. Practical application of these concepts, perhaps also as a response to increasing demands for accountability, came in United Way's decision to radically change the standards by which its local chapters can distribute their share of nationally garnered resources. United Way had traditionally based its funding on an internal evaluation of programs and services provided. But in 1995 United Way abandoned this method and decided to test outcomes, results, and program performance. Instead of looking at the quality, intention, or even high regard of its programs, the organization made the startling decision to test whether the programs had an impact, facilitated some change over time, or otherwise made a difference.

Within a few years, libraries followed suit. Soon after passage of the Government Performance Results Act, the Institute of Museum and Library Services (IMLS) focused on working with its grantees to measure the impact of their work through "systematic evaluation of results—outcomes." IMLS defines the process, known as outcome-based evaluation (OBE), as "a systematic way to determine if a program has achieved its goals" (IMLS 2000). Although grantees are not currently required to conduct OBE on their projects funded through IMLS, organizations are required to report to Congress in terms of measured outcomes. As the process of outcome evaluation becomes mainstream for government and other organizations, IMLS is sure to require its grantees to properly evaluate their projects for their success in achieving intended outcomes. Similarly, a 1998 update to *Planning and Role Setting*, titled *Planning for Results: A Library Transformation Process*, redirected public libraries toward outcomes-based evaluation. Instead of eight roles for public libraries, thirteen "service responses" were identified, and the new guide placed greater emphasis, perhaps because of the enormous technology and government changes taking place at the time, on obtaining and allocating resources. The planning guide was again updated and streamlined in 2001 with the publication of *The New Planning for Results* (Nelson 2001), which included two final steps: moving into the future, and informing stakeholders. "At its core," says the Public Library Association on its website, "*The New Planning for Results* is about managing change." All these shifts in our cultural, political, information, and community landscapes raise this question: Does what we're doing support our mission, provide value, and create change? A presentation introducing OBE (now available on the IMLS website) states: "Libraries Change Lives—Oh Yeah? Prove It!" We may still be far from what Larry White calls a "culture of assessment," but the culture of accountability, no matter what type of library we're working from, is upon us (IMLS 2002; White 2002).

Many libraries have found planning and managing for results, along with a comprehensive evaluation component, to be effective in telling the overall story of libraries and the difference we make for individuals and our communities. "Evaluation, believe it or not, can add to the excitement [of any new project] if it is done correctly" (Olney, Barnes, and Burroughs

2006, 1). If conducted systematically throughout a project, evaluation and planning can provide information for self-reflection and project improvement. It can also assist us in determining and articulating our value because it requires that we look at our bottom line and determine if what we're doing makes sense based on needs, resources, and the outcomes we've achieved.

If you would like further resources in this area, Kathleen de la Peña McCook offers a useful overview of standards, planning, and evaluation methods for public libraries that can help set context in *Introduction to Public Librarianship* (2004). Joseph Matthews tackles library evaluation models and methods in *The Bottom Line: Determining and Communicating the Value of the Special Library* (2002), *Measuring for Results* (2004), and other works (Matthews 2003, 2007; Matthews and Maxwell 2008). I. McCallum and S. Quinn review recent publications on the economic value of libraries in "Valuing Libraries" (2004), published in *Australian Library Journal,* and Leslie Fitch and Jody Warner provide an extensive bibliography of earlier work in *Dividends: The Value of Public Libraries in Canada* (1997). Roswitha Poll looks at ways of assessing economic and social value in "Measuring Impact and Outcome of Libraries" (2003), published in *Performance Measurement and Metrics.* Keith Curry Lance's Library Research Service is an online resource that includes multiple publications of library impact studies (www.lrs.org/impact.php). These resources and more can be found in the reference list and additional resources list at the end of this book.

HELPING LIBRARIES DEMONSTRATE IMPACT
An interview with Joanne Roukens

Tell us about your Valuing Libraries workshops. Why did you create them?

Valuing Libraries helps our member libraries develop powerful strategies for communicating what libraries offer their community or organization in terms of both quality of life and return on investment. My colleague Donna Bachowski and I created these workshops because we knew that libraries in the Highlands Regional Library Cooperative were struggling to tell their libraries' stories effectively. We then shared the idea with New Jersey state librarian Norma Blake. She funded the project so we could take it statewide. The Regional Library Cooperatives in New Jersey are multitype. We tried to make the workshops useful to public, school, and academic libraries. Every type of library can benefit from sending a representative to these workshops.

What do the workshops cover?

We focus on strategies and resources for qualifying and quantifying impact. We also work through creating a value proposition and provide a template for producing a simple return on investment calculation. By the end of the workshop, our participants are much more comfortable "pitching" their library story, making written and verbal cases to stakeholders, giving a one- to three-minute "elevator speech," and making a ten-minute presentation about their library.

How many people have taken the workshop? Have you been able to track the impact of the workshops on libraries in your area?

I estimate that we've trained over 300 library staff in this workshop since 2006. As a result, we've received some of the most positive and inspiring feedback from our participants who have immediately put the outcomes of our workshop to practical use in their communities. We collect evaluations from our participants—maybe it's best just to let some of their comments speak for themselves!

- "Valuing Libraries was an informative, inspirational, and practical two-part program that allowed me to bring definitive strategies and ideas to incorporate in my library immediately."—Rosemary Linder Day, Parsippany-Troy Hills Public Library System
- "I have wanted to prepare an ROI analysis for my library for a long time. Now I have completed it— thanks for making it so easy!"—Jane Fisher, Rutherford Public Library

- "This is the most useful, practical, and exciting workshop I have attended in thirty years."—Polly Lacey, Joint Free Public Library of Morristown and Morris Township

Is there anything else you'd like to say about the power of using these tools to tell your library's story?

All projects grow and change. Originally, the workshops were in two parts, two weeks apart, with homework in between. We've now created one-day versions, two- or three-hour versions, a workshop focused on the special needs of school libraries, and one for public library trustees. But they all still have homework! I've presented workshops not only in New Jersey but all over the United States and hope to do more. Libraries bring tremendous value to their communities, and their contributions can be demonstrated. With the Valuing Libraries workshop, we've tried to give our members the tools they need to make that demonstration. Libraries need to tell their funders and stakeholders that they are essential contributors to a community's quality of life and show them that the library is an incredible bargain.

Joanne Roukens is the executive director of the Highlands Regional Library Cooperative in Denville, New Jersey. Valuing Libraries workshop resources and working examples are available on the cooperative's website for anyone to use and share. Just go to www .hrlc.org/valuing_libs/valuinglibs.htm.

EVALUATION BASICS: RESOURCES, CAPABILITIES, USE, AND IMPACTS

Libraries have often operated under the auspices of public good and public will. In happy, bountiful times, when everyone is feeling prosperous, even generous, perhaps the motto Libraries Change Lives is good enough. Meanwhile, we've spent a lot of time counting—counting our resources, our processes, and our patrons' use of the library. Take these last two points together. We take for granted that Libraries Change Lives, and we believe, or perhaps hope, that the number of things we can count along the way will be enough to keep doors open when times are lean. We're learning now that counting alone won't do the trick. We've got a long way to go before we "prove it!" Meanwhile, libraries have focused on input and output measures and depended on these to tell the story of library value to community stakeholders. When confined to telling the story of what we have and what we do, communicated and perceived value is also constrained, leaving out entirely the story of why we matter. No matter how difficult they may be to pin down, impacts and outcomes go a long way to confirming the perceptions many have had of libraries for years—that they are worthwhile. Clearly the library's whole story is more compelling and can be more effective for making our case and improving our service toward meeting community needs. Instead of throwing current—however incomplete—evaluation efforts out the window and rushing into an outcomes-focused arena, consider balancing current efforts with selected measures from the areas we haven't paid much attention to. In this section I'll attempt to make some sense of all these various factors by pulling them together through the lens of community building.

First, let's go over a few definitions and a basic model for thinking about evaluation in libraries within the context of our progress in this area over time. Evaluation should be considered in context with the library's overall purpose and strategy. Very simply, every library should first have a clearly stated mission. A library's mission should be explicitly related to the values determined by the community the library serves, and if the community has its own mission statement, by all means, tie the library statement directly to it!

Next, the library should articulate a vision for accomplishing that mission or purpose, accompanied by strategies or plans that will get us there. Evaluation tells us how we're progressing along this path and gives us insight into ways to adjust for our future. From the community-building perspective, evaluation can help us (1) be accountable to our goals by indicating our progress toward meeting community needs, (2) tell a more compelling story about library value to all the stakeholders in our community, and (3) address future or necessary adjustments or improvements to library services based on our past performance and stakeholder buy-in.

In his book *Measuring for Results* (2004), Joseph Matthews discusses a general evaluation model first put forth by R. H. Orr in 1973. The model presents four basic components of evaluation: resources, capabilities, utilization, and impacts. Specific measures are associated with each component, and each type of measure has had its place in the progression of evaluation and planning models for libraries. Taken together they can tell a compelling story about a library's progress and performance in building strong communities. We'll spend a brief time on each, and then discuss how to pull them all together into a consistent method for evaluating library programs and services, in part or as a whole.

Resources are allocated to the library to complete its work. Resources are measured by *inputs,* and these measures are typically the easiest for libraries to gather. Inputs are resources the library has and include finances, collections, staff, systems, and facilities. Input data have been reported by libraries for decades and were once used by state library agencies and the American Library Association to develop minimum standards for library service. Over time, standards models were considered less useful than more inclusive planning models because they are unenforceable, do not include information about library activities, and are ultimately not complete measures of a library's overall performance. Input measures are still regularly collected and reported by public libraries through their state library agency as part of the mandate of the National Education Statistics Act of 1994. The National Center for Education Statistics (NCES) remains the most reliable source for descriptive data about public libraries as part of the Library Statistics Cooperative Program.

Capabilities are the ways resources are organized and managed so that library services can be provided. Capabilities are appraised by *process* measures that identify how efficiently resources are turned into actual services. These measures include cost and time required to deliver the service and can often point to areas where productivity and other types of efficiency can be improved. Process measures, like inputs, are focused on internal library activities and can include economic efficiency, staff productivity, and system reliability measures. Benchmarking—the process of comparing your process measures to the process measures of others in order to constantly improve—can be used to identify trends over time, set new performance goals, and show decision makers how individual libraries compare to one another.

Utilization describes how patrons or users interact with the library. Use is measured by *outputs,* which are related to patron use of the library (services, collections, systems, and facilities) as well as to patrons' satisfaction. The most typical output measures include circulation data, number of library visits, number of reference questions asked, and fill rates. Outputs can also measure perceived or actual quality of library services (accuracy, relevancy) and how they are delivered (timeliness, friendliness, approachability). As with inputs, some of these measures are descriptive and can be easy for some libraries to collect and report on. Others require staff to collect existing data, manually tally activities and users, or survey users. The planning resources for public libraries developed by the Public Library Association in the late 1980s took an important step away from the input-based standards models. These outlined output evaluation as the feedback part of the library planning process, where measurement was outlined in terms of data collection, analysis, and reporting. Because outputs go a long way toward describing current library conditions and activities and because they can often be quite impressive, they have been criticized when taken alone to describe the library's purpose and presence in their community.

A number of "single measure" library ratings systems (such as the HAPLR Index, www.haplr-index.com) have also been developed. Because they depend heavily on input and output measures, they have been criticized for some of the same reasons minimum standards have been (Lance and Cox 2000). According to their critics, input, process, and output measures can help us say, *The library has (and has done) all of this! Our library users have done all of that!* Left out is the final consideration of a comprehensive evaluation program: *why it matters.*

Impacts are the effects of library programs or services and are measured through *outcomes.* Impacts can be generally categorized as economic or social, and for individuals or groups. Economic impacts are quantifiable, or tangible, and can be quantified for individuals, organizations, and the community as a whole. Economic impacts include financial savings, increased property values, or increased revenues. Social impacts are intangible and refer either to the meaning or benefit the library has to individuals served (such as literacy, learning, or leisure), or to the collective social capital gained through a sum of interactions (such as democracy, engagement, and community building). Single individual, family, or organization impacts often become apparent in the day-to-day activities of library staff as they offer library services and are frequently reported as anecdotal or qualitative evidence for library performance in annual reports and day-to-day advocacy efforts. Outcome measures are relatively more difficult to formally assess in aggregate than input or output measures are, but pressures from the social sector have pushed many libraries to begin outcome-based evaluation for specific services and programs. In a broader sense, we've seen libraries striving to "demonstrate impact" or "communicate value" to individual library users, funders, and their communities at large.

Paying attention to each of these components, and balancing them in a mix of strategies for tracking your library's effectiveness toward meeting your mission and achieving your goals, will ensure a close connection to your community, informing new or improved services and collections to meet community needs.

EVALUATION BUILDS COMMUNITIES
An interview with Catherine D'Italia

What draws you to community building as a framework for library practice?

I spent twenty years working in the private sector. I was offered a short-term independent contract job to raise money for the creation of a space to house the library's historical materials collection. I took the low-paying job because I thought it was a gift to my community. The rest is history. Louise Blalock, our chief librarian, arrived in 1994 and began the gargantuan job of turning a traditional library into a model for how libraries can move beyond their doors and become part of the fabric of the community.

What are your library's long- and short-term goals for community building?

Community Development and Civic Services is one of seven programs of service that the Hartford Public Library (HPL) has developed to respond to the needs of the diverse community. We have a high degree of cross functionality among our staff and in the integration of seven key programs of service, all of which support the mission to promote and support literacy and learning, to provide free and open access to information and ideas, and to help people participate in our democratic society. The library functions under a Balanced Scorecard Logic Strategic Plan that was implemented in 2004 and that calls for evaluation according to four key criteria: *end results* for HPL customers and the Hartford community; *processes and practices* that enable HPL to serve customers well and achieve better results for the community;

learning and growth of HPL employees, systems, collections, and infrastructure to enable the library to change, grow, and improve its practices; and *leadership and engagement* in the community and region to identify needs that the library can serve.

Is there something you've worked on that you'd call a successful community-building project?

Our Neighborhood Teams' mission is to Listen, Learn and Link. The teams are made up of staff from a neighborhood branch with additional staff from our central library. Additional staff may live in the neighborhood, have expertise pertinent to the neighborhood (e.g., the health librarian is a member of the team in the neighborhood of the Hispanic Health Council), or otherwise be connected locally. The library developed this innovative program to be in better touch with community needs. The teams have existed for about ten years and are now a fixture in the community. Team members attend community meetings, and other library staff members attend community events and programs as well as make public appearances. In FY2007/08 library staff members attended 600 meetings; overall attendance at those meetings was 31,100. As a result, very few people in and around Hartford do not know what the library is doing and do not appreciate its efforts.

Did the project meet its goals? How was this measured?

The library has been recognized as a model for proactive community service. A report within a broad national study, "Approaches for Understanding Community Information Use: A Framework for Identifying and Applying Knowledge of Information Behavior in Public Libraries," identified Hartford as a "holistic and contextually driven service model" for anticipating community information needs. The Information Behavior in Everyday Contexts (IBEC) research team of Joan Durrance, Maria Souden, Dana Walker, and Karen Fisher identified the attitudes, practices, and strategies that allowed the Hartford Public Library to become an integral part of the community and an active community participant. The model of intervention that was developed at the library provides an increased ability to anticipate community needs. The HPL model shows how the various strategies used by the library work together and form a framework that serves to meet the needs and aspirations of library customers and community groups. This national study, a collaboration of the information schools of the Universities of Michigan and Washington, was funded by the Institute of Museum and Library Services, the government agency with oversight responsibility for museums and libraries.

If you could offer any advice to other library workers about community building, what would it be?

Commit to it—make it a high priority—the rewards are enormous!

Catherine D'Italia retired in 2008 after fourteen years in development and public relations for the Hartford Public Library in Hartford, Connecticut. You can visit the library on the Web at http://hplct.org.

EVALUATION FOR COMMUNITY BUILDING: IT'S NOT FOR THE MONEY, BUT THE MONEY IS NICE

Libraries of all types are grappling with increased expectations around evaluation of all kinds. We can rarely, if ever, complete holistic evaluation programs with input, process, output, and outcome measures in balance. Instead, funding agencies, governments, departments, supporters, management, or even tradition will dictate the cycle that most of us go through annually: missions and values are reviewed; community needs are identified; plans are made and implemented; measures are gathered and analyzed; communications deliver the news or the story to stakeholders; new budgets are allocated; adjustments to library services drive the cycle for the coming year.

Why Evaluate?

The critical motivator in this cycle, sometimes for better and sometimes for worse, is funding. Budgets allocated for the following year often depend on the library's ability to effectively communicate or prove its value to decision makers and other stakeholders. From this perspective, evaluation can seem overbearing or even despotic. Shifting our perspective slightly away from the demands of securing continued funding as our primary motivator and returning to our initial mission and purpose as a library may make our evaluation program more meaningful to our communities as well as less burdensome to library staff. In short, "the library must be able to identify and communicate how it adds value to the lives of its users and the quality of life in its community," not to ensure funding—although that may be an additional outcome—but because we're ultimately accountable to our communities and to ourselves for the work we do in libraries (Matthews 2004). In their book *How Libraries and Librarians Help,* Durrance, Fisher, and Hinton note that evaluation can help librarians "speak a common language with other agencies about their contributions to civic engagement and community life and to articulate to key audiences the vital and unique role that libraries play in civil society" (2005, 21). The authors also note that intentional evaluation can augment and support our planning, marketing, and sustainability efforts.

> Knowing outcomes, librarians will find themselves empowered to improve strategic planning and narrate the library story. They will be better able to equip themselves to compete for scarce dollars. By infusing marketing vehicles like presentations, reports, newsletters, flyers, and bond issue campaigns with evidence of their services' impact, librarians will send strong, consistent messages of their *value proposition* for their communities. By publicizing the positive outcomes we also place emphasis on identifying negative outcomes, which provide invaluable feedback for improving existing services and initiating new ones. (Durrance, Fisher, and Hinton 2005, 22)

Similarly, in their work *Evaluation and Library Decision Making* (1990), Peter Hernon and Charles R. McClure point out how evaluation efforts relate to planning, service delivery, and sustainability. Their list of evaluation benefits includes more appropriate organization goals, program objectives, and resource allocation, as well as discontinuance, fine-tuning, or new innovations in library services and activities. Moving beyond funding as the primary motivator, evaluation efforts support all our community-building activities in libraries and provide support for the other elements of the community-building process.

Selecting Measures

Once we've shifted to a community-building perspective, our first opportunity to build community through evaluation lies in the space between developing strategic plans to meet community needs and selecting our measurements to identify our progress toward that end. With clarity about community needs and about plans and strategies to meet those needs, selecting evaluation measures that identify the library's progress toward meeting those needs becomes critical. We can also choose to evaluate one or more projects or services, one or more service areas, or the library overall. Starting small and then expanding your evaluation effort as you learn over time is perfectly reasonable. When you're ready to take it on, overall performance can be evaluated in the combination of measures collected, enabling the library to tell a complete story about its resources, activities, processes, use, and impacts. Don't let the number of things you *could* do with evaluation paralyze you from evaluating at all. Instead, focus on a few key measures in each area and for each program, and then for the library overall. The keys are aligning measures with activities and goals and balancing our selections so that we tell a more complete story. In time, and as you learn, you can take on more and more ambitious efforts. Pulling all these measures together into a single plan provides the framework, or logic model, for evaluating library services and programs. Review books and articles by Joseph Matthews and by Joan Durrance and Karen Fisher for more detailed instructions on complete general and outcomes-based evaluation models. It may also be useful to draw on recent planning and evaluation efforts when designing your own programs. Keith Lance built on public library efforts to evaluate the impacts of special projects funded by the Library Services and Technology Act (LSTA) and developed a model for evaluating overall public library services (based on the Public Library Association's thirteen service responses listed in *Planning for Results*). *Counting on Results* (Lance 2002) includes instruments for recording observed patron activities as well as collecting patron-reported impacts of interactions with library services. In *Measuring for Results* (2004), Matthews offers an illustration for overall performance measurement that selects aspects of each component and balances them among types of measures.

Perpetual Iteration

We can also build community through evaluation in the space between analyzing our selected measures and improving or adjusting library services. When we're able to better answer the question, *What difference did we make?* we bring clarity to how well our strategies and activities were able to meet community needs. Specific suggestions for adjusting services in our next cycle then come to light. Planning future iterations, together with revised needs assessment as necessary, can direct library managers toward consistently more relevant library services. Attending to these lessons, as well as continually checking in with the community we seek to serve, ensures that our services stay meaningful and that we remain accountable for service efficiency and quality.

SUSTAINABLE OUTCOMES

An interview with Christopher Jowaisas

What are the core elements of a sustainable library?

The most important element is engagement with the community at multiple levels—in the environmental scan, in the refinement of programs and services, and in finding out what is working and what needs to be improved. Having a library that is willing and able to do this means implicitly that you have strong leadership. It also means having (not as implicit, but still needed) an operational mind-set that focuses on actually pulling off what is proposed, or at least the willingness to try to do that. It is the realization that it is not the library staff's library, but the community's library. You also need some way to measure and display progress, both internally and externally, to the stakeholders—staff, other community leaders (political and social), citizens, and potential funders. This helps keep everyone focused on why you are doing certain things and understanding the risks and challenges of trying to accomplish them.

Why do you think we're seeing conversations about "sustainability" rather than "funding" in our professional discourse? Is there a difference?

I think we have seen this shift in many places because library leadership realizes that they have to take in the scope of the situation—and that funding is only one piece of that puzzle. Your funding could actually be going up or keeping pace with cost increases and yet you could still not be building a sustainable organization. I guess I would break it down into the old saw about thinking strategically versus thinking tactically. Increasing funding is a tactic; building a sustainable set of services that meet community needs is a strategy.

How do you see the social enterprise movement fitting into this discourse? Do you think libraries are being asked (in a general sense) to do the same things that nonprofits are?

Generally, yes, they are being asked to answer many of those same questions: Why should I give my money to your organization versus another? What do you add to the community that is unique or valuable? Libraries themselves have a tremendous well of social capital that they have built up that they are still drawing on, although they have drawn more heavily on it in the past twenty-five years and it is running out in many areas of the country. Similar to what is happening in many nonprofits, I think people want to not just give money, but they want to lend expertise (e.g., Social Venture Partners, www.svpseattle .org), but libraries struggle with how to do this beyond the typical volunteer roles. One possibility is the role of Superpatron (e.g., Ed Vielmetti's site, http://vielmetti.typepad.com/superpatron/), but because of the way many of our main technology systems are constructed, this really does require a Superpatron. In the future, we need to think about how we can tap our community's passion for the library and use that latent talent pool to improve the services that we provide to the community. Lately, I have been wondering how we improve our operational processes and who libraries can tap in their communities that have this type of expertise.

If this is a permanent shift, or at least a steady trend, do you think libraries can cope?

To me it is unclear whether most libraries can or will. If by cope, you mean operate at the same level of subsistence, then of course they can. If you mean are they going to be thriving organizations in their communities, I think that is up in the air. I think a general change in how we approach determining and presenting our value to the community has to happen. Accountability is definitely more common at all levels—we ask our grantees for outcomes and other measures so that we can demonstrate impact to our funders (the federal and state governments). But I do not think that most libraries have made that shift completely—look at the struggle to implement some type of measurement and planning tool like outcomes-based evaluation. This is due to several reasons: one, many of our services are not well suited to being measured in this way; two, it requires a fair amount of resources to do outcomes measurement; and three, it requires a mind-set that focuses on planning and asking whether the services are delivering the results that we planned. For many libraries, this is beyond their capacity to begin with, but instead of searching for another way to answer this question, they fall back on standard output measures that don't tell the story of their impacts. So often what I see is that libraries can't seem to wrap their minds around how to present the amazingly compelling work they are doing in a framework that resonates with others outside the organization. I always say that we seem to be deaf to the "value vocabulary" of others.

People want to hear the story of how you are impacting people's lives and know that while you are doing that, you are keeping a watch on the resources and trying your best to eke out the maximum benefit for those dollars. I think for some libraries they either want to keep their heads down and not even be noticed or they fall back on the whole "but we're really important to democracy and apple pie and all that good American stuff and kids come and read books" without actually getting into why that is any better than other services or how it improves the community, yet they could make those arguments with a focused effort.

And I do not think this is necessarily new, but has been heightened because in some communities we're seeing a lack of support for libraries. Why do people not vote for the tax increases for libraries? Basically it boils down to not seeing why they should. In many places the thick veneer of "it's good" that used to surround libraries has been chipped away at over the years through a variety of forces, and now it is no longer there and libraries, for the most part, are lagging behind in adjusting what they are doing to operate in this new environment.

Are there other things, beyond the inability to articulate value, that lead to lack of community support?

Fear is one. I think of success as much as failure. And in taking the "safe" path of change. I see it in my work often—basically, let's do a scan of needs and then just slot our existing programs and operations into that framework without addressing those needs. And let's not analyze a service to see if it is cost-effective as long as it is new or splashy. I see libraries choose to fund a service that gets used by .01 percent of the population and has little if any demonstrable value to the community, yet costs tens of thousands of dollars annually, and I wonder how that can be justified when another program—say, emergent literacy, workforce training, or small business development in cooperation with other entities in their region—would be a much more powerful story to tell when they come around for funding next time.

The libraries that are willing to give up what they want to do in order to do what needs to be done—which in many cases is probably harder and less glamorous—and that have the leadership to tackle that challenge will thrive, will be sustainable. But it's easy to keep putting up barriers and providing the minimal set of services and hiding behind the excuses. Getting out of our comfort zone—personally or organizationally—is a hard thing, but so often when we do, it leads to good stuff. Even getting people to think about the library in a new way is a challenge, especially when we have been doing a good job of providing services on limited budgets. Recently I heard a director discuss how she was looking at a news article about the funding cut at another library and realized that even with the cut that library was taking, if her library had the same per capita funding as that library, her budget would double. When she told this story at the city managers' meeting, one of them asked,

"Yeah, well, aren't your patrons happy now?" She replied that they were because the library is very focused on providing good customer service and programs aligned with the needs of the community, but that the patrons have never experienced the full range of services that could be provided with a good level of funding, so they were happy because they were ignorant of what opportunities are out there. I think that is another piece of the puzzle of challenges that we face—how do we inspire our communities with a vision of the services, their value, and then mobilize the support to provide those services above what we are doing now?

Can you give us an example of a library you think is sustainable?

Douglas County, Colorado. I have not worked with them personally, but I have talked with and read stuff by their director, Jamie LaRue, and I think he is building a sustainable library. Jamie seems to understand that he has to have one foot firmly planted in the intellectual "I wanna do good with my library" world and one foot in the "how do I figure out how to sell this to people who want to believe in a good story and then support it?" world. He is very cognizant of the realities of funding; his library is funded through an operating levy that has to be renewed every six years, so he has to keep his ear to the ground to figure out what his community's needs are and how he's going to meet them.

Christopher Jowaisas is currently working as a grants administrator at the Texas State Library and Archives Commission. You can visit Chris's sustainable library pick, Douglas County Libraries, online at www.douglascountylibraries.org.

The final community-building opportunity uncovered by this research lies in the space between gathering measurements and communication. Taking great care to manage or balance our strategies and measures with effective communications can position the library to better demonstrate to both users and decision makers how they meet community needs and, perhaps more important, attract or retain sufficient resources to keep the cycle going. Engagement with stakeholders can help us make the case to funders that our services are accountable, are trustworthy, and merit additional investment. Community engagement will convey and ensure renewed commitment to our purpose and mission: to meet the needs of the community we serve. But none of this matters if we're not in it for the long haul. Many of the librarians I worked with on this project talked about sustainability, which we'll discuss further in the next chapter.

NOTE

1. See New York (www.nysl.nysed.gov/libdev/helpful.htm), Florida (www.flalib.org/publications_tab_files/FL_Pub_Lib_Standards _5_7_08.pdf), and Colorado (www.cde.state.co.us/cdelib/ Standards/pdf/PLStandardsFinalCopyALLSeptember7.pdf) for a few current examples.

CHAPTER SEVEN

Sustain

The future sustainability of libraries will be in making sure that the community is aware of what libraries can do for them. Free, common meeting places are necessary for all ages.

—Robyn Hammer-Clarey, Whitehall Public Library

Maybe because I spent more time with academic libraries, I am a rookie when it comes to community involvement. I always took libraries for granted growing up, and even while working in them, I tend to feel we have a built-in audience. My current position is the first time where community outreach is heavily stressed, and it is an eye-opener. Libraries are no longer taken for granted, and taxpayers are asked many times to renew millages to pay for library services. It seems that librarians should have to take political science, urban planning, and marketing courses just to meet the communities' needs.

—Randy Farb, Flint Public Library

ASSESSMENT, DESIGN, ENGAGEMENT, AND EVALUATION, even when pulled together into single projects or long-term plans, are not enough to keep communities connected, their libraries open and vibrant. Another essential element of successful community building is thinking about the long term. Sustainability accounts not only for how current resources are deployed in order to discover and meet community needs but also for how future resources will be ensured toward the same goals. In its broadest terms, sustainability refers to the processes, resources, and efforts required to create and maintain a balanced, ideal state. And although sustainability appears at the end of our discussion, it is not the final component of a successful community-building project; rather, it should pervade every aspect of our service. But what, exactly, has sustainability got to do with building community? Let's take a look at a few definitions and the emergence of the term as it relates to community building and libraries.

Typically associated with environmental protection, the concept of sustainability was first applied to development in the late 1980s. Norwegian Prime Minister Gro Harlem Brundtland defined sustainable development in 1987 as development that "meets the needs of the present without compromising the ability of future generations to meet their own needs" (World Commission on Environment and Development 1987). In 1992, the United Nations established the Division for Sustainable Development and, over the past two decades, has established the concept of "sustainable development" as contingent on three interrelated factors (also called the three pillars): the environment, society, and the economy. The term has been criticized as a misnomer, particularly as economic and environmental factors relate to one another, and for its reliance on traditional notions of "efficiency" in regard to the economy. Regardless of the critique, as we've moved into twenty-first century, the discourse around sustainability continues to reach out into other disciplines and is now being applied to institutions and organizations across both private and public sectors. Researchers and theorists recognized that policies related to environmental, social, and economic factors were not sufficiently impacting overall sustainability. The organizations and institutions implementing policy and creating change must also be sustainable themselves.

Institutional sustainability entered our professional vocabulary in large part because of the Bill and Melinda Gates Foundation's focus on sustainability for libraries. Midway through its five-year U.S. and Canadian Libraries programs, and while placing 40,000 computers in 11,000 libraries, the foundation's field trainers and tech support staff started to ask serious questions about the longevity of the foundation's overall investment in libraries. *Library Journal's* 2000 Public Library Budget Report noted, for example, that

> many of those same libraries that were so exultant two and three years ago may find themselves in a technocrisis when the Gates grants end and they are left to their own financial devices to maintain net services and to implement upgrades. Nearly nine of ten libraries will see their Gates funding run out in FY00, which means they will have to devise new ways to raise cash to make up the difference. Libraries in poorer jurisdictions face stiffer challenges, particularly with net-related expenditures increasing in libraries across the board by an average of 15 percent. (St. Lifer 2001, 406–7)

With staff turnover increasing, hardware and software growing tired, and many libraries poorly positioned, financially and otherwise, to continue to support their public access computing programs, the foundation began to engage libraries in additional conversation, training, and planning. The goal was for libraries, and especially their public access computing programs, to become sustainable on their own. As part of its Staying Connected grants, the foundation fulfilled more than twenty library-related grants explicitly citing sustainability as their main purpose. These grants were largely bestowed on state library agencies acting on behalf of the library staff that they serve. Meanwhile, other foundation grantees were increasingly called upon by the foundation to initiate and implement their own sustainability plans. Staying Connected grants now completed, the foundation has partnered with the American Library Association to complete the Public Library Funding and Technology Access Study. The purpose of the project in part is to uncover "the impact of public library funding changes on connectivity, technology deployment and sustainability" (ALA 2006). With these and other projects, the foundation can impact library sustainability at the institutional (rather than organizational) level.

Capacity-building for self-sustainability has reached beyond the institutions to the organization and individuals. Another part of the Gates Foundation's interest in library sustainability and public access involves its development of the first online peer-based network for library staff. Originally funded by the Gates Foundation, WebJunction is a learning community for library staff that offers anyone working in libraries the ability to set up a profile, connect with colleagues, ask questions, report problems, contribute and share solutions, and participate in training or professional development courses, webinars, and events (www.webjunction.org). The site infuses its web and workshop environments with a supportive and welcoming atmosphere so that even the least tech-savvy library staff members feel comfortable asking questions, sharing insights, and otherwise contributing. In 2005, WebJunction launched its Rural Library Sustainability Project, also funded by the Gates Foundation, which put librarians representing rural libraries around the country together in workshops and at conferences to discuss the competencies related to creating vibrant rural libraries. Reaching across institutions, organizations, and individual library staff, the most current and critical conversation in our profession is shifting from technology, access, management, or even patron services to, very simply, our own sustainability.

So what's at stake for librarians as community builders? In short, we're increasingly accountable as individuals, organizations, and institutions to our funders, supporters, and other community stakeholders for our own strategic planning, ongoing assessment of both needs and impacts, community engagement, and the resources we're using to pull it all off! The Bill and Melinda Gates Foundation's encouragement of its library-related grantees to develop and implement their own sustainability calls into question the reliance of many library service agencies, and even libraries themselves, on the philanthropy of both public funding and their various benefactors. With traditional sources of funding as much in question as library programs, services, and practice, our challenge is to look beyond traditional funding models without compromising our social purpose. With intention around sustainability, all our activities begin to answer this challenge: are we effectively managing our resources, for now *and* for our future, so that we *can* fulfill our social purpose? If you're already thinking about it, you're well on your way to answering yes!

NOTHING IS IMPOSSIBLE
With Cynthia Fuerst

The small town of Kankakee, Illinois, is a diverse community of about 30,000 people, comprising about 45 percent African American, 45 percent white, and 10 percent Hispanic residents. We are located about fifty-five miles south of Chicago and about seventy miles north of Champaign-Urbana. We were a struggling community (rated last in the 1999 *Places Rated Almanac*), but we are rebounding (our rank went up significantly in the 2007 *Cities Ranked and Rated*). We are a city library, which I think may give us an advantage. We work closely with the city administration and aldermen, as well as with the other departments of the city (police, code, fire, public works, etc.). Our library's goals support the city's goals. We partner with anyone who will work with us—schools, businesses, social agencies, county government, other libraries, other communities, and the like.

Our biggest and most successful project is our new library. We worked with the city and a private developer to renovate the first three floors of an existing office building to house the public library; the top four floors remain private office space. We desperately needed a new facility. Our 10,000-square-foot, 100-year-old building was woefully inadequate for our community of 30,000. We hired a consultant to do a needs assessment in 1996, which led us to hiring a person to evaluate the fund-raising potential of our community in 1998, which in turn led us to talking with the private developer who was considering building an office building. It is a long story with many ups and downs, but basically that same developer approached us at the beginning of 2004, and we opened our doors in January 2005. Ultimately, the city came up with the funding—$5 million—and the council doubled our levy to support the new library. No one has complained about the funding, because the new library is three times as large, with five times the computers. Use tripled in our first year after opening and continues to grow!

This project has really impacted the downtown. Several new businesses have popped up since our arrival—two new banks, a coffee shop, an insurance company, and more. Even the Friends group has increased from roughly 20 to over 150. In June 2006, we were honored by Pulitzer Prize–nominated author Luis Alberto Urrea, whose *New York Times* Op-Ed piece "Kankakee Gets Its Groove Back" outlines his unexpectedly positive experiences visiting our library and community. "Kankakee is pulling itself back from the brink," Urrea claims, "and it all started with the library." The community is really proud of its library. Everyone from the city mayor to our patrons will tell you so. I believe that ongoing use will be the key to how we measure our success. It is beyond anything we expected.

What I learned from this project: *nothing is impossible*. Building community isn't just about money. You have to make the best of what you have and think outside the box. Utilize everyone on your staff, from the shelvers to the board members. They know the community, what people are talking about, what is popular, what is needed, what will go over well with their neighbors.

At the time of this writing, Cynthia Fuerst was the director of the Kankakee Public Library in Kankakee, Illinois, where she debated and discussed with her assistant director on their blog (http://lions-online-shesaidhesaid.blogspot.com). In January 2009, she moved on to the Vernon Hills Area Library in Lincolnshire, Illinois.

FROM CONCEPT TO PRACTICE: PURPOSE, LEADERSHIP, ACCOUNTABILITY, PARTICIPATION

Libraries and other institutions are struggling with the shift to sustainability as much as they are with technology and management issues in libraries. Sustainability may seem an obscure concept that's difficult to put into practice, but exploring some examples of organizations working to bring sustainability principles and practice into their operations (both in libraries and other fields) helps focus some of the key elements of library sustainability. In other sectors, sustainable organization is linked to corporate citizenship, accountability, best practices, social responsibility, and social enterprise. Although library missions are often already associated with social responsibility and public good, we can still learn from the experiences of organizations striving to relate their missions (often, to produce profit for stakeholders) to social good. With social good increasingly associated with our own funding (if not revenue) generation, perhaps we can all learn from one another. Still a new area of interest and discussion, the following elements of sustainability planning give us a few approaches to consider.

Identifying Purpose

Where is your library now? Where do you hope to be in the future? What is your library's purpose and commitment to your community, and how is this valuable to them? As we discussed in chapter 5 on library program and service development, strategic planning includes a library mission and vision, usually established by the library director, board, and staff. Stating clearly and succinctly your library's vision for your community, how that vision relates to community needs, and your organization's mission to fulfill that vision can help identify how to best allocate library resources (for staff time, collections, programs, and other services), as well as how all library activities help achieve library goals. The mission of your library should identify the library's purpose and explain why it exists. The language should be clear and speak to your whole community; it should also be focused on the present and clearly invoke actions for both library staff and patrons. Mission accomplished? Let's look at the other elements of sustainability planning.

Democratic Leadership

With a multitude of stakeholders at the table, it's critical to include the voice of each partnering organization or institution you're working with. For Heiko Leideker, executive director of the Forest Stewardship Council (FSC) and 2005 winner of the $1 million Alcan Prize for Sustainability, "there is no shortcut to real participation in the system to truly involve everyone in the decision making." Recognized for its cross-sector work with forest industrialists, environmental stakeholders, and social constituents on how forests should be managed and protected, the FSC is another example of partnership created out of a history of conflict and contention. The conflicts were ultimately resolved with shared commitment to democratic decision making. Decisions aren't unanimous, but are derived by consensus. "All decisions made by FSC," explains Leideker, "are based on equal votes from northern and southern [hemisphere] interests and from environmental, social, and economic interests. No one interest can dominate a decision" (Schweitzer 2005).

In our community-building work at WebJunction, we've learned that (cliché or no) you can't just build it and expect them to come. Identifying teams, partners, and common needs and interests and creating open communication and relationships among stakeholders *doesn't just happen, even once you've set the stage.* Early on, individual ownership of the network's process, communications, and even team logistics (that you might otherwise think of as an afterthought) are critical to sustaining our intentions and to carrying out ongoing tasks. Leadership, in this sense, refers not to the declaration "Here's where we're going. Follow me!" but instead to an ongoing process of creating and holding the container for other voices and roles to emerge, to witness and document individual responsibilities, and to keep the group moving forward through your process. "One thing I tell people who are interested in applying the model to their sectors or industries: You are committing to an open-ended process," says Leideker of the FSC. "Only to a certain extent is it predictable as far as where the process will go and what outcomes will result. Conflicts arise for which there is no particular template for resolution. It takes a lot of courage" (Schweitzer 2005). When there is no consensus and all voices have been heard, leadership asks those with outstanding opposition to get on board anyway.

As the Rural Library Sustainability Program trainers in Kansas, Cindi Hickey and Brenda Hough learned that leadership is critical to the success of their project, even though it was well supported financially, with additional resources and structure and with committed participants (see the text box "Sustaining Rural Libraries"). Their leadership in this project focused on and enabled the networking, sharing, and connections with colleagues across the state needed to develop and deliver on sustainability action plans there. Patrons and library staff in Kansas are now reaping the rewards!

SUSTAINING RURAL LIBRARIES
With Cindi Hickey and Brenda Hough

Librarians serving in Kansas's small and rural libraries face so many challenges—shrinking budgets and rising costs, increased patron demands for new services and information access, competition from bookstores and online resources, and rapid change. In many cases, continued service to patrons in our rural areas may depend on librarians' abilities to sustain their services, information access, and technology. The curriculum for WebJunction's Rural Library Sustainability Project focuses on principles that can help librarians frame their sustainability strategies. These principles include planning, community involvement, local solutions, advocacy, and outreach (to both the local community and the library community). Kansas participated in this program in the winter of 2006. Participants in Kansas's workshops worked with sustainability principles and created action plans for their libraries aimed at sustaining their library's technology. They left the workshops to go back to their communities to refine and implement their plans.

To sustain our own work in this program, Kansas sustainability trainers developed three goals:

- Foster continued connection and networking among our workshop participants to help reduce their isolation and provide a forum for discussion and sharing.
- Encourage participation in the WebJunction Kansas community by leading our participants to resources that specifically support this sustainability project.
- Offer opportunities for practicing with some of the social online technologies that help people connect with each other.

To meet these goals we created a strategy for regular follow-up along with three separate approaches to staying connected. First, we established a blog titled *Building a Sustainable Future,* now available as *BlogJunction Kansas,* at http://webjunctionworks .org/ks/blog/ to introduce our participants to blogging and to provide leads to WebJunction events, resources, and support for the workshop curriculum. The blog allows interaction through public comment and retains the information for future access. We also established an e-mail list for our participants hosted by our library school. The list allows us to send out meeting notices to everyone and to post blog entries to encourage our participants to visit the blog. Finally, we scheduled monthly one-hour follow-up meetings using a web-based conferencing program offered by the Online Programming for All Libraries (OPAL) consortium. Based on Voice over Internet Protocol (VoIP), this meeting space allowed us to connect with our participants from our desktops. Each month we offered a program (blogging, TechAtlas, planning, etc.) and time for sharing and discussion.

Through the workshops and the follow-up sessions, we were inspired by the tireless efforts our librarians make to sustain their libraries and, through that, their communities. Small libraries with one- or two-person staffs provide patron computer training on topics from using e-mail to e-mailing photos to using eBay. One librarian partnered with the sixth-grade teacher in her local school to match students with seniors for one-on-one e-mail training conducted and practiced at the library. Other librarians set aside money each month for a technology fund to cover computer replacement. Another librarian has partnered with an English instructor at a local community college to provide monthly writing classes. The students write on the library's computers, and their writings are compiled by the library. Action plans from some of our other librarians included using WebJunction's courses for staff training, developing relationships with schools that offer equipment and Internet service, and creating partnerships with local computer stores and Internet providers that trade technical support and Internet access for promotional considerations. The best part is, all of our workshop resources are available on the website so that other librarians across Kansas can learn and benefit from these experiences. All these efforts help librarians build local relationships that result in local solutions, which may be the bed-rock of library sustainability.

Cindi Hickey is the WebJunction coordinator and continuing education librarian for the State Library of Kansas. Before joining the State Library she served as the coordinator for the Institute for Continuous Education (ICE) at the School of Library and Information Management, Emporia State University.

Brenda Hough is the technology consultant for the Northeast Kansas Library System in Lawrence, Kansas, and a doctoral student in the School of Library and Information Management at Emporia State University. She moderates the InFocus rural library webinar series on WebJunction and the WebJunction Emerging Technologies discussion forum.

Demonstrating Accountability and Contribution

The economic aspects of library sustainability are twofold: (1) the community resources required to run library services, facilities, and programs, and (2) the contributions the library makes to its community. The former involves stewardship: the careful acquisition, disbursement, and accountability for our funding and other resources. (See chapter 6 for more on the "culture of accountability.") The latter involves carefully accounting for and articulating the ways we give back. Both are important for sustainability in libraries.

In her book *The Thriving Library* (2007), Marylaine Block explores the essential qualities of libraries that have earned the enthusiastic support of their communities. Twenty-one out of twenty-nine library directors surveyed by Block stated that "stressing the economic value of the library" was critical to their success in creating a library thriving with ongoing support from the community. Stressing economic value was ranked sixth after service to teens, defining public space, courting community leadership, building partnerships, and marketing. Block's research also revealed that successful library directors publish financial records and annual reports online as well as generate alternative (non-tax-based) funding, complete cost-benefit analysis, serve the business and nonprofit communities, and track the library's contribution to revitalization, local spending, property value, and overall economic development. After building a new central library in downtown Seattle, the library partnered with Berk and Associates to publish *The Seattle Public*

Library: Economic Benefits Assessment; The Transformative Power of the Library to Redefine Learning, Community, and Economic Development. The study explains that the library was responsible for new net spending of $16 million during its first full year of operation, that nearby businesses reported increases in spending associated with tourists and visitors to the library, and that library and library resource use increased dramatically across the city.

FRIENDS GROUPS HELP WITH FUNDING
with Rebekkah Smith Aldrich

The Mid-Hudson Library System in New York State (MHLS) is a library consortium with sixty-six autonomous member libraries. As an agency devoted to supporting public libraries, we see great value in supporting others with our same mission—Friends groups. More than half of our libraries have active Friends of Libraries groups, and in 2005 our system started reaching out to them. We began with a Friends recognition event—Friends Matter—to bring Friends from around the system together and to thank them for their dedication to their libraries. The event was a huge success. We realized this was a segment of library supporters hungry for help. They ranked meeting fellow Friends as the most helpful aspect of the night. People noted it was interesting and fun, but they were looking for practical information.

> "As a new Friend you have made me quite excited about the possibilities of what Friends groups can do. I found out that there's a lot more I need to learn about Friends."—Friends Matter 2005 attendee

Over the next two years, we developed resources for Friends, a portion of our website was dedicated to resources for Friends, and our long-standing fund-raising list became the "Friends and Fund-raising" list, devoted not only to fund-raising tips and grant sources but to best practices for Friends. I began offering consultations to Friends as I do our members—from getting started to planning for fund-raising to managing volunteers and obtaining tax-exempt status.

Our second Friends Matter event addressed the calls for inter-action and practical information. Participants engaged in a Friends Café, which consisted of three roundtable discussions led by a combination of Friends and MHLS staff that focused on just one question: How can Friends groups help build community support for libraries? Highlights from the discussions included the follow-ing:

- Have a shared vision with the library board about the role of the Friends.
- Have a strong mission statement for the Friends.
- Be educated about what resources and services the library has to offer.
- Help to create a "buzz" in the community about the library.
- Be visible.
- Participate in nonlibrary community events and provide the opportunity for others to become a Friend during community events.
- Assist the library in reaching out to new residents—sponsor a Welcome Bag, conduct tours of the library.
- Help broaden the library's program offerings for kids and adults.
- Participate in the chamber of commerce breakfasts.
- Create a Friends website to promote the good work of the Friends.
- Help the library publish a regular newsletter and an annual report to the community.

Because the Friends were ultimately looking for opportuni-ties to talk to their peers, we began the quarterly Friends Support Group. Friends from around the system come to meet and discuss (and eat!). We start with a topic and everyone joins in to share questions and solutions, frustrations and joys of supporting their libraries. Notes from the meetings are captured and shared on our website to reach those who aren't able to make a meeting.

"I think this opportunity to share with other 'Friends' is really helpful—it inspires us to keep trying."—Friends Support Group regular

With an abundance of resources gathered over the past two years, we redesigned the Friends portion of our website—it currently includes information about the types and purpose of Friends of Libraries groups, about how to get them started, and about their formation, revitalization, participant recruitment, and ongoing support. Sample mission statements, bylaws, brochures, and even memos of understanding between Friends and the library board have been collected for nascent groups to use. All our resources and support are designed to develop strong, lasting Friends of Libraries groups that help their libraries with advocacy, fund-raising, and volunteer efforts. We're proud of our Friends and the support they bring to libraries throughout the Mid-Hudson region.

> Rebekkah Smith Aldrich is the coordinator of member information for the Mid-Hudson Library System. Serving sixty-six member libraries, Rebekkah consults with library staff, trustees, and Friends on topics ranging from funding and construction to marketing and long-range planning. Visit the MHLS website to learn more: http://midhudson.org.

For libraries not currently thinking about sustainability, this collection of multiple strategies may seem overwhelming, especially if you try to tackle them all at once. But your first steps toward strategic stewardship might be supporting your Friends of the Library group (see the text box "Friends Groups Help with Funding"), applying for a grant, or simply changing the term *overdue fines* to *extended borrowing fees* and seeing what happens. At the Sanilac District Library in Port Sanilac, Michigan, using the different term meant a more positive attitude and maybe even an increase in library revenue! How's that for alternative funding!?

Demonstrating your library's contribution to the community can be as simple as pointing it out more clearly. Supporting local business might mean partnering with the chamber of commerce, or simply providing reasons for patrons to visit local businesses. Serving local small businesses works for Jean Workman, director of the F. D. Campbell Memorial Library in Bessemer, Pennsylvania. Jean involves small local businesses in some of her ongoing summer programs—for example, by including local businesses as stops during the library's teen summer bike scavenger hunts, after which the participants return to the library to collect their prizes. For a children's coloring contest, forms were distributed at local businesses, but completed drawings were collected at the library. Joint programs cost very little for either the library or local businesses, but generate traffic and visits for both. "Small libraries have a place in the scheme of things just like small businesses," says Jean. "We deal in service and caring to the people." Lee O'Brien's Small Business Information Center in Cecil County, Maryland, was established on the same principle: that libraries and small businesses can help each other (DelVecchio 2006).

A number of library-specific resources are available on securing and articulating the economic value of the library; you'll find some of these resources in the additional resources list at the end of this book. If you're just beginning to think strategically about the economic aspects of library sustainability, browse through a few of these resources to see which ones resonate with you and the information/capacity you currently have in your library, and start there. If you've already tackled a few of these strategies, look over these resources for some ideas you haven't tried that would work for your community.

BLOGS BUILD COMMUNITY (WITH PEOPLE I SEE EVERY DAY)
With Helene Blowers

When most people think about online learning communities they are typically thinking about people who are engaged in conversation and information sharing from remote and different locations. But online communities can be beneficial not only to those who are separated by distance or multiple zip codes; they can also bring people together even within the same organization or physical location. This was exactly the result that the Public Library of Charlotte and Mecklenburg County experienced with its groundbreaking staff development program, Learning 2.0.

The Learning 2.0 program was developed to help library staff gain exposure to and comfort with Web 2.0 tools by encouraging them to complete nearly two dozen small challenges, known as "23 things." The program differed from other popular online training formats and tutorials because it used the very same tools that it exposed participants to and in the process created a very powerful online learning network.

As a participant in the program, each staff member was required to create a blog and share his or her thoughts via posts about the discoveries made as each "thing" was completed. The richest learning experiences occurred through the peer blogging community, and it was exciting to see self-proclaimed tech novices become experienced Learning 2.0 tutors through simple exposure and "play."

The success of the program was best measured by the outcomes that were captured in the participants' comments, where learning themes were strong among all the final posts:

> "I guess the biggest 'take away' for me is that the 23 things forced me (in a good way) to expand my knowledge and now it's up to me to continue that learning process because there is so much out there to learn about and do."

> • • •

> "If it hadn't been for you and Learning 2.0, my knowledge of technology would still be in a very small box. Now my knowledge of technology has expanded to a not-so-very-small box. There's still lots to learn, but now I can't wait to learn more."

> • • •

> "I feel like Cinderella who just finished her chores in time to go to the Ball. (But the chores were a learning experience and hold promise for the future.)"

In the end, the nine-week program encouraged over 350 staff to join the learning and blogging network. A total of 226 completed all 23 things and, as many of their blog posts shared, their journeys turned out to be much more than just solo learning exercises; they created a peer-to-peer learning network. One participant said it well:

> "I have to say one of my favorite parts has been being able to check out [my coworkers] blogs to see what they did and get tips on how to complete the exercises. It was great to see all the variation in each of the 'things,' what people found, what they thought was interesting, what they decided to look at, or what they

created. Learning 2.0 has taught me a lot and now I'm hooked."

Helene Blowers is the coauthor of *Weaving a Library Web: A Guide to Developing Children's Websites.* She is most widely known as the architect of the discovery learning program Learning 2.0: 23 Things. Currently she is director of digital strategy at the Columbus (Ohio) Metropolitan Library. Online she can be found at http://LibraryBytes.com.

PROFESSIONAL RELEVANCE: STAYING IN TOUCH WITH OTHER LIBRARY PROFESSIONALS KEEPS *YOU* SUSTAINABLE

In *Bowling Alone,* Robert Putnam notes that both bonding and bridging social capital are critical for healthy communities. *Bonding* refers to the value assigned to social networks between groups of people who are mostly the same, and *bridging* refers to that of social networks between socially diverse groups. In a system where bonding social capital is not balanced by bridging social capital, self-serving or bullying "gangs" or intensely hierarchical acceptance systems can form and become a burdensome form of social capital. I find this distinction helpful for thinking about library staff generally and our overall relationships to the communities we serve.

Ranganathan identified, long before new media and the participatory Web swept through library practice, the bonding social capital that some library staff used to establish their own value relative to nonprofessionals and even to keep users from information resources that were considered rare or precious. These practices are again coming into question with the breakdown of the notion that the expertise of the library staff professional is more valuable or more important than other kinds of expertise in the library setting. Generally, I think this is a positive, though sometimes challenging, shift for the library practitioner. Most of the rest of this work and research has revealed the importance of bridging social capital that helps build communities. But sustainability and relevance of the library cannot be achieved through bridging alone. Also key are intention and attention to our need to refuel and recharge, to bond with our colleagues who have similar professional values and ideals. Balancing our bridging connections with the community with a substantial set of bonding connections to other library staff can also balance the trendy or even confusing array of options we have before us. An eye to the future is almost always best tempered with a balanced approach that includes making choices, focusing, and doing the most important things (not just doing things well). A mix of expertise and experience can bridge generation gaps even within a homogeneous group. Taking time for conferences, meetings, blogs, social networking sites, instant messaging, e-mail lists, online communities, mentoring programs, certification, or other types of professional development not only can help us stay connected to the communities we serve, it also can help us stay connected with one another. And the wisdom of *that* crowd is really something.

FIVE WEEKS TO A SOCIAL LIBRARY
An interview with Meredith Farkas

What do you think are the major challenges library staff face in their jobs in the coming year?

I think most librarians are incredibly busy. One major challenge we all have is making continuing education a priority. We have so many day-to-day responsibilities and wear so many hats, it's often difficult to justify going to a conference or reading an article when there are so many other things to do. However, continuing education is absolutely vital to our providing the best possible services to our patrons; how else can we learn about the latest trends in libraries or technologies available to us?

Tell us about Five Weeks to a Social Library. Why did you decide to do it?

Five Weeks to a Social Library is an online course designed by six librarians who wanted to teach other librarians who would otherwise not have access to continuing education about social software and how to apply social technologies in their libraries. My goal when I originally conceived of the course was to show others that high-quality online education programs could be designed on the grassroots level and without spending a lot of money. Although there were some required components, a lot of the material and activities were optional, so participants could do as much or as little as they were able to. All of the course materials were available after the course so students could later read or watch things they didn't have time for during the five weeks. I wanted to develop a sustainable model that others could replicate in the future to make online education more accessible to librarians. We designed the course to be an extremely rich and interactive experience, with participants not just listening to lectures and reading articles but blogging, chatting, and actually *using* social technologies. These active and reflective learning activities helped students really engage with the tools and consider how they could be used in their libraries. This is a course that could very easily be adapted for different groups, different subjects, and different time frames. With the exception of web conferencing software, all the tools used in the course were open source and therefore a cost-effective option for any institution.

How did you measure success for this project?

I think a course is successful if participants are able to take what they learned and apply it in their libraries. To evaluate the effectiveness of this course, we asked our participants to reflect on their learning experience (on their blogs in response to our questions), and their feedback was overwhelmingly positive. By simply reading our student blogs, we could also see that the majority of participants were really engaging with the course materials and tools and were questioning how these technologies could be used in their libraries. A number of the individuals in the class have already implemented social software tools in their libraries, either during or right after the course. Three months after the course, I plan to send out a survey to participants to find out what they've accomplished, in terms of implementing social software tools at their library since the course ended.

What's next for librarians who want to take an active role in their own professional development? Any predictions?

These days so many educational opportunities—blogs, webcasts, forums, and more—are now freely available online. At the same time, the technologies themselves have become more accessible. It's so easy now for anyone (without tech savvy) to start a blog, try a wiki, or play around with social bookmarking. The tools are all there for anyone to develop her or his own continuing education program; the only major barrier is finding the time. Fortunately, I think more and more libraries are looking at implementing in-house training programs, which will make continuing education more reasonable for library staff who are pressed for time, and this will help to build a real learning culture in the organization.

> Meredith Farkas is the distance learning librarian at Norwich University in Northfield, Vermont. In 2007, Meredith was the chair of Five Weeks to a Social Library, a free online course designed to teach social software to librarians who would otherwise not have access to this type of continuing education. You can follow Meredith's blog, *Information Wants to Be Free,* at http://meredith .wolfwater.com/wordpress/.

The Internet came to the library first as something that could help us connect with other professionals and help us connect patrons with materials. Our services in this space now help patrons connect with us and with one another, not only at the Internet access terminals that our libraries provide but also through (in the early years) the dial-up services we offered from home and the patron training programs that started with how to use a mouse or keyboard, extended to e-mail and Google, and now facilitate patrons teaching one another how to create videos and upload images to the Web. Reference has similarly moved to e-mail, IM, and collaborative digital reference services. Now we use blogs, social networks, and other forms of user contribution to connect both with patrons and with colleagues. If we can continue to find in ourselves the flexibility, adaptability, and tolerance for collaborative mush, but bring that together with some of the concepts and examples from different fields and disciplines, we'll be able to sort through the different ideas about what it means to be sustainable and see instead what these have in common: a focus on identifying purpose, common stakeholders, and needs; fostering intentional and democratic leadership; facilitating relationships; creating personal connections; and delivering on economic accountability and contributions. As you move into your next project in your library, consider sketching out your plans for engaging your colleagues, partners, patrons, and the community at large in your sustainability efforts and their involvement with these approaches in mind. Professional relevance is about more than simply keeping up with trends and opportunities. We all benefit and grow from learning and sharing together in networks common to library practice.[1]

NOTE

1. If you're looking for a place to start, you can join an existing
   community of other community builders (http://shell.cas
   .usf.edu/~mccook/alaet/), other "blended" librarians (www
   .blendedlibrarian.org), other 2.0 technology supporters (http://
   library20.ning.com), or other learning communities for library staff
   (www.webjunction.org).

AFTERWORD

Inside, Outside, and Online—
We Are Everywhere, and Should Be

OVER THE COURSE OF THIS WORK, I realized that librarians are building community inside, outside, *and* online. The presence and the practice of libraries and librarians are no longer bounded by our roles, our library type, our library size, or our geographic locations. We're not even bounded by our buildings or websites. And although the spaces where services are delivered are different, as are, presumably, the audiences there, ultimately the tactics and the practices put to use in these spaces and for these audiences are entirely common among them. The tools used to create connections within these spaces differ, however, and complement both the audiences and the spaces where they are used. If only the tools are different, perhaps the work of "new" or "2.0" librarians is built on and connected to their colleagues, both current and past.

Still, many librarians perceive a major divide, perhaps generational, between librarians building community inside, outside, and online. Although their practices are strikingly similar, their tools are different, and so there remains a perception that there is little in common between traditional and digital librarians. I hope this observation challenges these perceptions and facilitates the new and enduring connections necessary between librarians from all types of libraries, roles, and generations to build our own social capital for the advancement of objectives wherever they are shared.

I'd love to hear from you if you have further insights or thoughts to share. Visit http://librariesbuildcommunities.org to continue the conversation there.

Libraries Build Communities Online Survey— Selected Questions and Answers

Is there something you've worked on that you'd call a successful community-building project? Why was it successful? What lessons did you learn?

In 2008 we rolled out a learning 2.0 program (modeled on "23 Things") for 2,300 people (the public library workforce across the state, http:// nswpubliclibrarieslearning2.blogspot.com). One activity involved contributing to a wiki (http://nswpubliclibrarieslearning2.blogspot.com). You can see from the contributions people made—particularly the library assistant ones—how many people work in isolation or thought no one else understood what their job was like. So far more than 230 people have completed the course; considering it is completely self-paced and voluntary, we are pretty happy with progress to date. Many more are still working through it. Key lessons we have learned: a training program that can be delivered remotely can reach our whole target audience equitably; not everyone found it easy to operate in a virtual community, but many commented on how proud of themselves they were when they finished the course—someone even described it as life changing.

. . .

Our Blue Bag Bonanza was an incredible event, [held in conjunction] with Raising a Reader, Friends of the SFPL [San Francisco Public Library], OCYS [Office of Children's and Youth Services], and a neighboring child development center. Prior to the event, we processed new library cards for approximately sixty-five students and their parents, and after their mandatory parent meeting at the school site, I led them down the block to the library where we had a storytime, decorated library bags, and gave out the cards so that kids could check out their books. The bags from Raising a Reader are blue, so we had blue streamers, blue yogurt, blue spoons, blue water bottles. We had over 175 people in attendance—it was wonderful.

• • •

Looking ahead to your next few questions, I see that the expectations of this survey run to formal projects with clearly articulated, measurable goals and timetables for their achievement. That's fine for big projects—which I characterize as the Spanish Armada Approach—but we employ a much more immediate and casual approach of learning as we go—which I call the Dunkirk Model (find something that floats and start rowing right now)—[and] which generally lacks such quantification. We are about creating relationships by whatever means we can and then building on them over time, rather than entering into formal agreements with lots of management and measurement.

• • •

We have a Friends committee that does library displays, and they try to involve other community groups. We decided to do a display highlighting the local animal rescue organization, ACPaws. Someone suggested that we request donations for the group while the display was up. We turned it into a Dogs versus Cats contest to see who could raise the most money. It got a lot of publicity, and the competition between the cat lovers and dog lovers led to their involving others. We highlighted the contest in the newsletter and kept a running total. In the end, someone matched the total collected and said that they represented goldfish!

• • •

Reading Together just completed our fourth annual program. It was successful due to collaboration. A community-wide committee chooses the book, not the library. Depending on the book choice, the library convenes a steering committee of organizations interested in the theme.

Each year the committee has a different composition. The first year we read *Fahrenheit 451* and convened organizations interested in civil liberties, the arts, science fiction, etc. With *Nickel and Dimed,* we convened agencies that serve the working poor, homeless advocacy groups, etc. When we chose *The Color of Water,* the faith community, racial justice programs, memoir writers, and interracial families came together. This year's choice, *The Things They Carried,* struck a chord with veterans' groups and peace activists, among many others. We have learned that enlisting representative organizations that are stakeholders within the issue yields committed volunteers and makes for a dynamic program.

• • •

I am wrapping up my second year of "Hear and Say." It is a toddler storytime I developed, in which we work on the six skills of early literacy through PLA's Every Child Ready to Read program. It brings in mothers, fathers, grandparents, and other caregivers and gives them a chance to meet and get to know one another. We meet on Monday mornings, for six weeks (four sessions a year). It has been extremely successful. In fact this past session I had thirty sign up and a few more on a waiting list. Caregivers and parents in the community have been very responsive to this program because they want to give their child a head start into reading and literacy.

• • •

So far, our most successful program is Filmentality. We were able to involve several organizations that were doing similar things on their own and promote both this program and our other separate interests to a broader section of the community. People came to our film series who had never known that there was a community theater in Dowagiac so they got inside the building and perhaps will attend a play or become part of the theater in some way. The main lesson always is that everything starts much more slowly than you would like, and we needed to give the program a full year of monthly events before we built any sizable audience. Word of mouth was far more effective than any other advertising we did.

• • •

We had two days of poetry reading this past month. It brought faculty, students (cross division), and some parents together to share their favorite poems. This was great because it made the poetry come alive, and it used the space in a way it hadn't been used before. It's rare that the Big Kids get to see the Little Kids, and they really enjoyed the interaction. We'll do it again, but not on consecutive days, and try to get even more participation.

• • •

My Own Cafe is a teen web portal that Southeastern Massachusetts Regional Library System received an LSTA grant to develop for member libraries of the region. Its kickoff was this past February. It is a website for teens ages 13 to 18 in southeastern Massachusetts. Because it is still in its infancy, its success is yet to be determined. As of May 1, 100+ teens are on the site. The teens that are on the site are excited. There has been a lot of school/public library cooperation happening as teens need a library card to register. The project is still ongoing and we are still learning lots. We have had to rethink our perception of teens and listen more carefully to what they tell us. The website has created a "buzz" but it's really difficult getting libraries to join in on the "buzz." We are still working hard on this. Community is fragile at the beginning and needs much care and nurturing to keep it going at first. You need to have that dedicated few who keep the flames alive until the project develops its own life. This being a website for teens made safety real important to us. A few times it had me thinking what have we gotten into, especially as MySpace was making the news. We have been talking with our teen administrators about safety and language. It was just a matter of letting teens know that someone was available if there was a problem. There will be lots of little decisions that will have to be made despite the best planning—go with the flow when you can.

• • •

We have just completed our Learning Commons that includes partnerships with Faculty/Staff Technology Support, Student Technology Services, the University Writing Center (English Department), Speaking Center (Communications Department), Starbucks (Dining Services), Art Department (art gallery) and Photocopying Services. The partnership has been very successful, as it has provided us new partners and provided greater access for students to complete their academic projects. One of the lessons that we learned from the project is that when you begin a project like this, you never know where it will take you. The process began as a small lab of computers, and became something much larger. I think that this is the basis for many community-building projects.

• • •

We won an award last year for Operation Respect—and I was cited as a Mover and Shaker partially for getting it off the ground. This film discussion series led by well-known community figures was designed to address a hate crime that took place in our high school and succeeded in the number of people it drew in, the press coverage that followed, and the importance of the discussions it prompted.

• • •

An interesting program at a different branch in our system was the CSI-Louisville program (not a program I was involved in but is a benchmark that we use). Capitalizing on the popularity of the show, the librarians brought together forensic scientists, federal agents, and other interesting law enforcement individuals. The sheer fact that it had never been done before pulled in a far greater number than expected. Lessons learned: (1) plan events based on the audience in mind, (2) niche programming is not bad programming, (3) reach out for resources (get other organizations), and (4) if you offer something that no one else does, it will add that new, shiny edge to your program.

• • •

The youth services staff created, designed, and implemented Traveling Tales, an outreach program for child-care centers that can't bring their children to the library. It was hugely successful. It exposed both children and their caregivers to the library and its resources, and it put a face to staff. We learned the need is great for this kind of outreach and that more staff would be needed to fully implement it community-wide.

• • •

National Library Card Signup Month in September 2005 was a success for us. We did the classic library partnership, where we partnered with local businesses to give discounts to our patrons during the entire month. Thirty-two businesses participated. The businesses told us that library cardholders took full advantage of the discounts. Patrons used the local businesses and the library. In addition, we saw an increase in the number of new library cards added to the computer. We learned that you must start early, and preparation is the key. Begin coordinating very early. Publicity (newsletter, posters, banners, flyers, giveaways) for such events takes time to create.

What do you wish you could do to build community from your library, but don't feel you have time or resources for?

We need more online tools—wikis, forums, blogs, RSS feeds from our website, capacity to podcast seminars we hold at the library, vodcasting.

• • •

We need more space! Because our library is a historical building, we will likely not get more space . . . ever, but we would be able to achieve so much more! I'd also love to be able to offer literacy courses for our parents. They so often ask for that support, but we don't have the staff or space.

• • •

Provide more exploratory technology and a better way for patrons to give constant feedback about how they feel about the library and what they would like to change.

• • •

To have an FT position dedicated to community building, marketing, and public relations.

• • •

I would like to have a place in Second Life for working together with other social sciences librarians. I would like to make a contest—for the best library picture on Flickr. I would like to be in StudiVZ presented as a library.

• • •

More staff. It is a crunch to do outreach and staff the library in addition to the other tasks needed. Outreach is so important.

• • •

A new interest is in developing meaningful services for the boomer generation as they prepare for the next stages of their lives. Their needs and expectations will be greater than anything we've seen.

• • •

I wish I had more staff who were excited about getting people excited. And I also wish I had more staff who didn't view promoting the library to businesses as somehow not a core service. Over time, I will remedy that by hiring the right people.

• • •

It's not a matter of not having the time or resources, as those will naturally come as the overwhelming need to build and sustain these communities becomes increasingly apparent and moves into the library's SOP.

• • •

We are a low-income area with a lot of elderly. It would be great to be able to get out to them, especially in the winter.

• • •

More outreach. There are many organizations that we could work with and many issues on health disparities that could be covered. We are limited by staff size and budget in the amount that we can do. We'd like to offer funding to libraries to add staff to do this outreach as well, but again, funding is limited.

• • •

We would like to merge our library with the stand-alone City Arts and Culture Center (which rents space in the library) to streamline staff and better coordinate programs, services, staff, and facilities.

• • •

We can only do so much outreach. We want to do storytime in so many places but [it is] hard to coordinate schedules.

• • •

I'd like to start, or show people how to start, various "labor banks"—for instance, a babysitting bank where people take turns sitting for each other's children and earn credits. A lot of local people can't afford day care on minimum wage, so being able to trade off day-care time would help. Also, a "skills bank" would be good. Each person [offers his or her] skills for free and earns time to use other people's skills. For example, you paint my house and earn time, and then you cash it in for someone else to help sew your daughter's prom dress.

· · ·

I would like to reach more parents and students and get them excited about what we have to offer in the way of electronic resources. I want them to come to us first rather than Google! We are putting in IM for reference this fall, and I am hoping that this will be a new way to reach our young people and let them know we are here for their informational needs.

· · ·

I wish I could let more people know what we have to offer.

· · ·

A larger and more active Friends of the Library.

· · ·

I wish we could do more adult programming, get the children's book discussions back, and provide more YA resources.

· · ·

I wish we could be "out there" in the community more. Our users know what we do and how we do it, but of the 62,000 residents we serve, less than half have library cards. There are more than 30,000 people in the county that *do not* use us, and we need to figure out why, and figure out what it will take to get them into the library.

· · ·

I wish we could have a full-time librarian and children's librarian available for the bookmobile all week. Currently we run the bookmobile three afternoons a week with the children's librarian on it only one of those afternoons. Also, I feel that we need more staffing to meet the demands of our public without burning out our staff. This would also allow us to do more programs and storytimes.

· · ·

More programming for youth. Their options seem to be limited but this is a difficult age group to engage as well. The few things we tried this year were not well attended.

. . .

Faster Internet services. Currently we have a dial-up Internet connection.

. . .

Have more time and resources to make the other four cities more aware of all that we have available for them at this library. Have more collaboration with the schools and senior center, reach out to the business community too.

. . .

Positive contacts with local schools, especially new teacher orientation to the public library and joint planning with SLMS [school library media specialist]. Dedicated space in the building for literacy tutors and homeschooling families.

. . .

Spanish-language materials for both English speakers and native speakers.

. . .

I wish we could do more outreach into the community, and I wish we had the space to offer more community-building programming on-site.

. . .

Reaching out to the businesses of the community to let them know how we can support them and enhance their business.

. . .

Book clubs.

. . .

Generate community-based research projects in collaboration with local nonprofits.

. . .

Generate an out-of-schooltime volunteer/internship program for students.

. . .

South Africa has communities living in shared spaces that are very different economically from each other; for example, in our city the areas where those who cannot meet their basic needs exceed the areas (and cross over them) where quite well-off people live. However, children attending school (those that are lucky enough to do so) all have to achieve the same level of literacy to complete their assignments and final exams. As you can imagine, these children all face quite different challenges. Some find it easy; they have a place to work, a computer, a desk, privacy, time, access to libraries, tutors, and other resources. They are fetched and carried by their parents as well as having the support of adults. Others have none of these advantages and have never seen a study guide or a computer, don't have electricity or warmth, etc. It would be nice to even things out a bit by providing all students with the help they need. It would be nice to be able to provide reading material and information also to little children and their parents/caregivers.

. . .

It would be really great if our community members (and here I include the campus staff as well as folks from outside the campus) knew that we welcome them to the building and that many of our resources are here for them to use in-house as well as to borrow. Short of advertising, I'm not sure how that would happen. I'd like to be able to offer instruction and programs, and we're working toward that but are not there yet. My administration supports this, though, and I have an outreach committee to help out.

. . .

This website has demonstrated the need for our libraries to reach out on the Web—it would be great to adapt this site for other ages, such as adults. We also see a need for simple searching for library resources—a step beyond federated searching, where our resources are as easy to get to as Google. These are still on our to-do list.

. . .

I'd like to be able to meet with every business and organization in town on a regular basis, but unfortunately, I haven't figured out how to be in two places at once.

. . .

Enlarge the library and use Scott Bennett's *Libraries Designed for Learning* as a blueprint for planning, bring in the writing center and faculty development center, and make sure we can get a good cup of coffee without leaving the building.

• • •

Everything.

• • •

The town is badly split into factions. The library has participated in some "leadership" forums to try to alleviate the situation and to get more, less-divisive townspeople involved. We are unsure as to how to proceed without getting identified as part of one faction or another.

• • •

Offer more opportunities for social gatherings, like ice cream on the lawn in the summer, etc. . . . no money!!

• • •

We would like to branch out beyond the walls of our libraries to build communities in the living spaces of the students and the faculty departments that we work with.

• • •

We would love to draw high-caliber speakers, authors, artists to the library to inspire our town. Currently, we are applying for grants whenever we can, but this process takes time and resources itself. It would be wonderful to be able once a quarter to draw the town (all ages) together to some sort of "blockbuster" program about an issue or involving a performance that opens our minds to the world around us. Our community reads of the last two years have served that purpose, but we need to do more.

• • •

Getting out there more helps, but lack of staff is problematic. Not all librarians are the "get-outdoors-and-talk-to-people" type and so that can be a hurdle.

• • •

More outreach not only to child-care centers but to hospitals and senior centers. I believe all ages could benefit from library staff visiting and presenting programs, especially if they can't come to us. I'd also like to be able to offer outreach collections and homebound service.

If you could offer any advice to other library workers about community building, what would it be?

Web 2.0 skills are as critical as being skilled in searching the Internet was five years ago.

. . .

Join a community of committed community builders: http://shell.cas.usf .edu/~mccook/alaet/.

. . .

Community building is paramount! If not successful, try, try, try, try, try, try again!

. . .

Have an open discussion. Open discussions with patrons and staff will provide the best feedback and path to great services. The more you know about the needs, the faster you can provide the services.

. . .

To break out of the traditional library mold of "If you build it, they will come." Reach out and connect physically and electronically.

. . .

Take one step at a time. Do not be discouraged if schools or other organizations don't respond to overtures immediately. Sometimes it isn't the right time for them. Ask again.

. . .

Remember that 24/7 you *are* a representative of the library and can use that to your advantage and be an involved advocate. Get out there! Make connections!

. . .

Don't give up because one [project] might not work out when you have so many others that are so successful. Just keep plugging away until it works.

. . .

Libraries, like all human endeavors, are all about relationships and the thematic, economic, geographic, and/or familial clustering of relationships we call communities. Relationships are not necessarily expensive to create and maintain, but are essential to the health of the organization. A good understanding of the philosophy of marketing (not advertising, but husbanding the organization's many different exchanges with its publics— i.e., relationships) is the basis of success. The Web opens all sorts of exciting possibilities for creating relationships, if [it is] seen as an interactive, participatory platform and not some arcane, expensive technical subject best left to IT and Administration.

. . .

Get out there and talk to people! Walk down the street and stick your head into the shops and say "hi."

. . .

Don't give up. It takes several years for any new library service to take root and either succeed or not. Even if it is not a "success," you learn from each endeavor. Technology is changing so quickly, libraries need to be agile enough to evaluate it quickly and work with other libraries to share expertise and the time it takes to create a service.

. . .

Be willing to take part in the community. The more contacts you make, the more resources, support, and users result.

. . .

Think big, think why not, don't worry about the money, it will come, success breeds success.

. . .

We try to always go the extra mile, to never let anyone leave the library without an answer or the promise of one to come. We do things that aren't our job and see that as an opportunity to impress a voter with how great the library is as a community resource.

. . .

Get to know your community leaders. Make contact with groups and organizations with compatible missions and ask how the library can help. If your library has meeting space that is available to the community, take advantage of the opportunity to link with groups who are using the space. If you learn about community initiatives/projects/task forces, etc. to which the library has not been invited, don't shy away from advocating for the library to be "at the table." In other words, don't hesitate to be proactive. We started out by being the initiator more often than the responder.

. . .

Somewhere along the way we reached a tipping point . . . now organizations are coming to us asking us to be their co-sponsor/partner.

. . .

Sometimes we have to make the first step. When I came to work at the library, we had very strained relations with the historical museum. As a former museum curator, I made it a point to visit there and get to know the new director and archivist. This has really paid off for everyone concerned. I don't think we can wait for others to come to us.

. . .

The only advice I have to offer is to get out there and make yourself known. Find things that you can do to partner with others in order to bring many more people into awareness of the library and the contribution it makes to the community.

. . .

Talk to anyone and everyone, everywhere. Get involved in a community group, and at every chance, talk about the library. I'm new to town, so every chance I get, I'm introducing myself to business owners, vendors, salespeople. Even the folks I rent my apartment from know where I work. That could be super handy when it's time to start asking people for ideas, input, support, or even money. I've found, too, that sometimes simply asking "hey . . . how can we work together?" has opened up dialogue and helped build up a rapport.

. . .

Be involved in your community outside of work. I am a member of the Flint Club, an organization striving to promote Flint. I also attend city meetings, etc. on how to build a better community.

. . .

Don't give up—it takes much longer than you would expect. The results are worth it and can be very different from what you expected. The biggest thing we heard at the library was that people did not know we had audio and video materials—not just books.

• • •

Projects have always been much more involved than I ever initially expect and take longer than I think they will. I thought the local history project would be done in two board meetings and up and running in a month. Even though a project may take a while longer than I plan, it is a real help when it is finally working and the library patrons are satisfied that they got the information they needed and feel glad this is their library.

• • •

White Lake is a perfect example of a growing community that has no natural community center—there is no traditional downtown, and shopping is spread along the linear magnet of a state highway rather than being more naturally attracted to housing clusters. The library, especially in its location next to a small township park, has a core function—we are the only public agency in town that serves all residents. We are working hard to play up our role as community and cultural center, featuring such things as our regular Art @ the Library rotating gallery. That role as cultural and community center is not a natural connection for many Americans . . . who have inherited the idea of libraries as quiet places for students and old folks. Being very aggressive in our marketing will be the right answer for us; after years of just being here, we are now trying to be very very very visible. We believe that our future, both as a library and as a community, depends upon that active voice.

• • •

Just do it. Scale it down to what you can manage and can afford, but just do it.

• • •

Keep busy and look actively for potential partners. I've been able through the fund-raising professionals group to link up with the hospital in a closer fashion, and we are exploring more joint programs for the future.

• • •

You need crazy volunteers and crazy librarians to make good things is my personal opinion. If you'd like to have project plans, a lot of managers, and so on, it's going [to be] very slow and the workers [will] lose their enthusiasm on the way . . . Not always maybe, but . . .

• • •

Take small steps. Don't feel you need to get it 100 percent right the first time—anything is better than nothing and perfection will come in time. Too often we get caught up in the "we *must* do _____" and forget that even the small things count.

• • •

Do anything you can with the resources you have. Grant write, grant write, grant write!!!!

• • •

Treat each library member as an individual with distinctive needs. A real variety of information coupled with an egalitarian approach seems to work well. Treating children especially with dignity and respect gives them the chance to interact on an equal footing and share information about their literacy experiences and expectations. Always ask questions.

• • •

It's a long, long process. It's also a continual process. Don't get discouraged and keep meeting people and talking to them all of the time. I always keep my business cards handy, and I try to go to places where I think I might meet the folks I want to lure into the library!

• • •

My advice is to be flexible and open in the process as you try to reach out in the community. You will find that one idea might be great but not feasible or that something else is more important to that community. The end result is worth the effort. The sense of pride that the participants have is so great to see. Several of our teens came to our legislative breakfast this year and to hear a shy person come forth and say My Own Cafe is my favorite website was such a reward for those of us who nurtured this idea along. Also there were times in its initial development when we wondered if the interest for the site was waning—and we just had to pick it up ourselves and keep moving along. When community happens you tend to forget all those moments of doubt.

• • •

Read Bennett. Libraries should be about the people they're for, not about the services we think they need. Make sure there's nothing that inadvertently makes some people feel not at home or not welcome. And relax about food.

• • •

Pick an area/organization/project and concentrate on doing it well. Spinoffs will happen . . . go with them.

• • •

Keep on building on what you have and update older programming constantly.

• • •

Don't think small! Make the most of the library's unique position in the community as a safe and nurturing venue for civil discourse.

• • •

If you are a community librarian, your job never ends. I met the admissions officer of a local university at 10:00 p.m. in the deli at Wal-Mart! Learn about your city and stay with the pulse. What is unique and what tugs at the local people's hearts? What bothers them? A Rolodex, Internet connection, phone, and sense of humor are crucial tools when researching, talking, and making contacts with community leaders.

• • •

Keep trying. If something doesn't work, figure out why and retry. Write grants for start up funds. Tap the skills and knowledge of your staff to bring out their skills and interests so you have buy-in and desire to continue something that's been started.

• • •

Get out from behind your desk and go out into the community. Network with local organizations and businesses and build relationships. Use those businesses' expertise to help build community. Other businesses have customers. Make their customers your customers too!

Join the conversation at http://librariesbuildcommunities.org.

REFERENCES

Ahonen, Tomi T., and Alan Moore. 2005. *Communities dominate brands: Business and marketing challenges for the 21st century.* London: Futuretext.

ALA American Library Association. 1956. *Public library service: A guide to evaluation, with minimum standards.* Chicago: American Library Association.

——. 2006. Gates Grant Program. Press release. www.ala.org/ala/pressreleases2006/october2006/GatesFoundationgrant.htm.

——. 2007a. The state of America's libraries report (April). www.ala.org/ala/newspresscenter/news/pressreleases2007/march2007/stateoflibraries.cfm.

——. 2007b. New data on U.S. libraries shows almost two billion served (April 16). Press release. www.ala.org/ala/newspresscenter/news/pressreleases2007/april2007/salpr07.cfm.

Augst, Thomas. 2001. American libraries and agencies of culture. *American Studies* 42 (Fall): 12. Quoted in McCook 2004, 49.

Bajjaly, Stephen T. 1999. *The community networking handbook.* Chicago: American Library Association.

Baker, Sharon L., and Karen L. Wallace. 2002. *The responsive public library: How to develop and market a winning collection.* Englewood, CO: Libraries Unlimited.

Berk and Associates. 2005. *The Seattle Public Library central library: Economic benefits assessment; the transformative power of a library to redefine learning, community, and economic development.* Seattle, WA: Berk and Associates. www.spl.org/pdfs/SPLCentral_Library_Economic_Impacts.pdf.

Bertot, John Carlo, Paul T. Jaeger, Lesley A. Langa, and Charles R. McClure. 2006. Public access computing and Internet access in public libraries: The role of public libraries in e-government and emergency situations. *First Monday* 11 (9). http://firstmonday.org/issues/issue11_9/bertot/index.html.

Bertot, John Carlo, Charles R. McClure, Susan Thomas, Kristin M. Barton, and Jessica McGilvray. 2007. *Public libraries and the Internet 2007: Report to the American Library Association* (July). www.ii.fsu.edu/projectFiles/ plInternet/2007/2007_plInternet.pdf.

Bill and Melinda Gates Foundation. 2006. Needs and assets assessment worksheet. Promoting Public Libraries [workshop]. www.webjunction.org/ home/articles/content/442263.

———. 2008. Opportunity Online grants help public libraries improve quality of free computer access used by millions of Americans (July 15). Press release. www.gatesfoundation.org/press-releases/Pages/libraries -opportunities-online-grants-080715.aspx.

Block, Marylaine. 2007. *The thriving library: Successful strategies for challenging times.* Medford, NJ: Information Today.

Boase, Jeffrey, John Horrigan, Barry Wellman, and Lee Rainie. 2006. *The strength of Internet ties: The Internet and e-mail aid users in maintaining their social networks and provide pathways to help when people face big decisions.* Pew Internet and American Life Project (January 25). www.pewInternet.org/ pdfs/PIP_Internet_ties.pdf.

Bourdieu, Pierre. 1986. Forms of capital. In *Handbook of theory and research for the sociology of education,* ed. J. G. Richardson. New York: Greenwood.

Brown, John Seely, and Paul Duguid. 1996. The social life of documents. *First Monday* 1 (1). www.firstmonday.org/issues/issue1/documents/.

———. 2000. *The social life of information.* Boston: Harvard Business School Press.

Brown, William M. 2008. Future-proof design: Building for relevance and flexibility can ensure your library will be there to help patrons navigate rapidly changing times. *Library Journal* (September 15). www .libraryjournal.com/article/CA6593532.html.

Bryson, John M. 1995. *Strategic planning for public and nonprofit organizations: A guide to strengthening and sustaining organizational achievement.* San Francisco: Jossey-Bass.

Butler, Pierce. 1951. Librarianship as a profession. *Library Quarterly* 21 (October): 235–47. Quoted in Richard Rubin 2004, 248.

Coleman, J. C. 1988. Social capital in the creation of human capital. *American Journal of Sociology* 94:95.

Cornwall, Daniel. 2007. Armed Forces Medical Library closing? *Free Government Information* [blog]. April 4. http://freegovinfo.info/node/1051.

De Rosa, Cathy. 2005. *Perceptions of libraries and information resources: A report to the OCLC membership.* Dublin, OH: OCLC. www.oclc.org/ reports/2005perceptions.htm.

De Rosa, Cathy, Joanne Cantrell, Andy Havens, Janet Hawk, Lillie Jenkins, Brad Gauder, Rick Limes, and Diane Cellentani. 2007. *Sharing, privacy and trust in our networked world: A report to the OCLC membership.* Dublin, OH: OCLC. www.oclc.org/reports/sharing/default.htm.

De Rosa, Cathy, Lorcan Dempsey, and Alane Wilson. 2004. *The 2003 OCLC environmental scan: Pattern recognition; a report to the OCLC membership.* Dublin, OH: OCLC. www.oclc.org/reports/escan/default.htm.

Dees, J. Gregory, Peter Economy, and Jed Emerson. 2001. *Enterprising nonprofits: A toolkit for social entrepreneurs.* Wiley Nonprofit Law, Finance, and Management Series. New York: Wiley.

DelVecchio, Steve. 2006. "Building Partnerships Success Stories." www .webjunction.org/funding-strategies/articles/content/440069.

Dowd, Nancy. *The "M" Word: Marketing Libraries* [blog]. http://themwordblog .blogspot.com.

Durrance, Joan C., Karen E. Fisher, and Marian Bouch Hinton. 2005. *How libraries and librarians help: A guide to identifying user-centered outcomes.* Chicago: American Library Association.

Edwards, Bob, Michael W. Foley, and Mario Diani. 2001. *Beyond Tocqueville: Civil society and the social capital debate in comparative perspective.* Civil Society. Hanover, NH: University Press of New England.

Farr, James. 2004. Social capital: A conceptual history. *Political Theory* 32 (1): 6–33.

Field, John. 2003. *Social capital.* Key Ideas. London: Routledge.

Fitch, Leslie, and Jody Nyasha Warner. 1997. *Dividends: The value of public libraries in Canada.* Toronto: Book and Periodical Council.

Gates Foundation. *See* Bill and Melinda Gates Foundation

Girvin Strategic Branding and Design. 2002. King County Library System and University of Washington: Virtual reference services; marketing guidelines. www.secstate.wa.gov/library/libraries/projects/virtualRef/textdocs/ MarketingGuidelines.pdf.

Godin, Seth. 2006. *Flipping the funnel: Give your fans the power to speak up.* http://sethgodin.typepad.com/seths_blog/files/FlippingNOpro.pdf. E-book.

Gorman, Michael. 1995. Five new laws of librarianship. *American Libraries* 26 (8): 784.

———. 1998. *Our singular strengths: Meditations for librarians.* Chicago: American Library Association.

Griffiths, José-Marie. 2004. *Taxpayer return on investment in Florida public libraries: Summary report.* Tallahassee: State Library and Archives of Florida. http://webjunction.org:980/wj/documents/8495.pdf.

Gupta, Kavita, Catherine Sleezer, and Darlene F. Russ-Eft. 2007. *A practical guide to needs assessment.* Pfeiffer Essential Resources for Training and HR Professionals. San Francisco: Pfeiffer/Wiley.

Halpern, David. 2005. *Social capital.* Cambridge, UK: Polity.

Hart, Keith. 1999. *Putting marketing ideas into action.* The Successful LIS Professional. London: Library Association Publishing.

Hernon, Peter, and Charles R. McClure. 1990. *Evaluation and library decision making.* Information Management, Policy, and Services. Norwood, NJ: Ablex Publishing.

Hill, Chrystie R. 2005. Everything I need to know I learned online. *Library Journal* (February 15). www.libraryjournal.com/article/CA502019.html.

———. 2008. What we need. *Library Journal* (October 1). www.libraryjournal.com/article/CA6598080.html.

Himmel, Ethel E., and William James Wilson. 1998. *Planning for results: A public library transformation process.* Chicago: American Library Association.

IMLS Institute of Museum and Library Services. 2000. *Perspectives on outcome based evaluation for libraries and museums.* Washington, DC: Institute of Museum and Library Services.

———. 2002. Libraries change lives—Oh yeah? Prove it! Presented at the Arizona Library Association Conference. www.imls.gov/ppt/PLA-02-2OBE.pps.

Kendrick, Terry. 2006. *Developing strategic marketing plans that really work: A toolkit for public libraries.* London: Facet.

Koontz, Christie M., Dean K. Jue, and Bradley Wade Bishop. 2008. Why public libraries close (June 30). www.webjunction.org/facilities/articles/content/11041525.

Kotler P., and G. Zaltman. 1971. Social marketing: An approach to planned social change. *Journal of Marketing* 35 (3): 3–12.

Kranich, Nancy. 2001. Libraries create social capital. *Library Journal* (November 15).

Lance, Keith Curry. 2002. *Counting on results: New tools for outcome-based evaluation of public libraries.* Washington, DC: IMLS.

———. 2008. Library Research Service [website]. www.lrs.org/impact.php.

Lance, Keith Curry, and Marti A. Cox. 2000. Lies, damn lies, and indexes. *American Libraries* 31 (6): 82–84, 86–87.

Lauterborn, R. 1990. New marketing litany: 4 P's passe; C words take over. *Advertising Age* (October 1).

Levin, Driscoll, and Fleeter. 2006. *Value for money: Southwestern Ohio's return from investment in public libraries* (June 22). Economic Benefits of Public Libraries. www.9libraries.info/docs/EconomicBenefitsStudy.pdf.

Lieberman, Michael. 2007a. Voters reject levy to fund Jackson County libraries. Dark Ages remain. *Book Patrol* [blog]. May 16. www.bookpatrol.net/2007/05/voters-reject-levy-to-fund-jackson.html.

———. 2007b. The demise of the Jackson County Library System. *Book Patrol* [blog]. October 3. www.bookpatrol.net/2007/10/demise-of-jackson -county-library-system.html.

Madden, Mary. 2003. *America's online pursuits: The changing picture of who's online and what they do.* Washington, DC: Pew Internet and American Life Project.

———. 2006. Internet penetration and impact. Washington, DC: Pew Internet and American Life Project. (April 26). www.pewInternet.org/pdfs/PIP _Internet_Impact.pdf.

Madden, Mary, and Susannah Fox. 2006. *Riding the Waves of "Web 2.0."* Washington, DC: Pew Internet and American Life Project (October 5). www.pewinternet.org/pdfs/PIP_Web_2.0.pdf.

Matarazzo, James M., and Lawrence Prusak. 1990. Valuing corporate libraries: A senior management survey. *Special Libraries* 81 (2): 102–10.

Mathews, Brian. *The Ubiquitous Librarian* [blog]. http://theubiquitouslibrarian .typepad.com.

Matthews, Joseph R. 2002. *The bottom line: Determining and communicating the value of the special library.* Westport, CT: Libraries Unlimited.

———. 2003. Determining and communicating the value of the special library. *Information Outlook* 7 (3): 26–31.

———. 2004. *Measuring for results: The dimensions of public library effectiveness.* Westport, CT: Libraries Unlimited.

———. 2007. *The evaluation and measurement of library services.* Westport, CT: Libraries Unlimited.

Matthews, Joseph R., and Lynne Maxwell. 2008. The evaluation and measurement of library services. *College and Research Libraries* 69 (4): 391.

May, Meredith. 2007. Largest library closure in U.S. looms: Federal funding dries up, leaving 15 branches in Oregon county on brink. *San Francisco Chronicle* (March 4). www.sfgate.com/cgibin/article.cgi?file=/ c/a/2007/03/04/MNGC7N6Q3M1.DTL.

McCabe, Ronald B. 2001. *Civic librarianship: Renewing the social mission of the public library.* Lanham, MD: Scarecrow.

McCallum, I., and S. Quinn. 2004. Valuing libraries. *Australian Library Journal* 53:55–70.

McCarthy, E. Jerome. 1960. *Basic marketing, a managerial approach.* Homewood, IL: R. D. Irwin.

McClure, Charles R. 1987. *Planning and role setting for public libraries: A manual of options and procedures.* Chicago: American Library Association.

McCook, Kathleen de la Peña. 2000. *A place at the table: Participating in community building.* Chicago: American Library Association.

————. 2004. *Introduction to public librarianship.* New York: Neal-Schuman.

McGeachin, Robert B., and Diana Ramirez. 2005. Collaborating with students to develop an advertising campaign. In *Real-life marketing and promotion strategies in college libraries: Connecting with campus and community,* ed. Barbara Whitney Petruzzelli. Binghamton, NY: Haworth Information Press.

Monroe, Margaret Ellen. 2006. *Margaret Monroe: Memoirs of a public librarian.* Madison: Parallel Press, University of Wisconsin–Madison Libraries.

National Social Marketing Center. 2000. What is social marketing? www.nsms .org.uk/public/default.aspx?PageID=10.

Nelson, Sandra S. 2001. *The new planning for results: A streamlined approach.* Chicago: American Library Association.

Oder, Norman. 2007. Jackson County, OR, library likely to reopen, with fewer hours, under LSSI. *Library Journal* (August 22). www.libraryjournal.com/ article/CA6471026.html?rssid=220.

Oldenburg, Ray. 1989. *The great good place: Cafés, coffee shops, community centers, beauty parlors, general stores, bars, hangouts, and how they get you through the day.* New York: Paragon House.

Olney, Cynthia A., Susan Barnes, and Catherine M. Burroughs. 2006. *Getting started with community-based outreach.* Planning and Evaluating Health Information Outreach Projects, booklet 1. Seattle, WA: National Network of Libraries of Medicine, Outreach Evaluation Resource Center.

Orr, Richard H. 1973. Progress in documentation: Measuring the goodness of library services; a general framework for considering quantitative measures. *Journal of Documentation* 29 (3): 315–32.

Owens, Irene. 2002. *Strategic marketing in library and information science: A selected review of related literature.* Binghamton, NY: Haworth Information Press.

Pew Internet and American Life Project. 2008. Who's online (a frequently updated table showing the current demographics of Internet users). July 22. www.pewInternet.org/trends/User_Demo_7.22.08.htm.

Poll, Roswitha. 2003. Measuring impact and outcome of libraries. *Performance Measurement and Metrics* 4 (1): 5–12.

Preer, Jean. 2001. Where are libraries in *Bowling Alone? American Libraries* 32:60–63.

Putnam, Robert D. 1995. Bowling alone: America's declining social capital. *Journal of Democracy* 6 (1): 65.

————. 2000. *Bowling alone: The collapse and revival of American community.* New York: Simon and Schuster.

Putnam, Robert D., Robert Leonardi, and Raffaella Nanetti. 1993. *Making democracy work: Civic traditions in modern Italy.* Princeton, NJ: Princeton University Press.

Quan-Haase, Anabel, et al. 2002. Capitalizing on the Net: Social contact, civic engagement, and sense of community. In *The Internet in everyday life,* ed. Barry Wellman and Caroline A. Haythornthwaite. Malden, MA: Blackwell.

Ranganathan, S. R., P. S. Sivaswamy Aiyer, and W. C. Berwick Sayers. 2006. *The five laws of library science.* New Delhi [India]: Ess Ess Publications (orig. pub. 1931).

Rettig, Marc, and Aradhana Goel. 2005. Designing for experience: Frameworks and project stories. Presentation for UX Week 2005 [conference]. http:// darmano.typepad.com/for_blog/rettiggoel.uxWeek.8.25.05.pdf.

Rubin, Richard. 2004. *Foundations of library and information science.* New York: Neal-Schuman.

Sandy, John H. 2008. Interior decorating offers a way to connect with patrons. *PNLA Quarterly* 72 (Summer): 4. www.pnla.org/quarterly/Summer2008/ PNLA_Summer08.pdf.

Schweitzer, Carole. 2005. Six degrees of sustainability. *Association Management* 57 (6). www.asaecenter.org/PublicationsResources/AMMagArticleDetail .cfm?ItemNumber=11250.

SLA Special Libraries Association. 1993–2000. *The impact of the special library on corporate decision-making* (1993); *Special libraries: Increasing the information edge* (1993); *The value of corporate libraries* (1995); *Valuing special libraries and information services* (1999); *Valuing information intangibles* (2000). Washington, DC: Special Libraries Association.

St. Lifer, Evan. 2001. "LJ Budget Report: The library as anchor." *Library Journal* (January). Quoted in J. Buschman, *Dismantling the Public Sphere* (Westport, CT: Libraries Unlimited, 2003), 58.

Stevenson, Siobhan. 2007. Public libraries, public access computing, FOSS and CI: There are alternatives to private philanthropy. *First Monday* 12 (5). http://firstmonday.org/issues/issue12_5/stevenson/index.html.

Urban Libraries Council. 2007. *Making cities stronger: Public library contributions to local economic development.* Evanston, IL: Urban Libraries Council. www .00urbanlibraries.org/files/making_cities_stronger.pdf.

Wallace, Linda K. 2004. *Libraries, mission, and marketing: Writing mission statements that work.* Chicago: American Library Association.

Warncke, Ruth. 1974. *Analyzing your community: Basis for building library service.* [Springfield]: The Illinois State Library and the Illinois Library Association.

Whelan, Debra Lau. 2008. Three Spokane moms save their school libraries: How three women from Spokane saved their school libraries and created an advocacy model for the rest of us. *School Library Journal* (September 1).

White, Larry Nash. 2002. *Does counting count: An evaluative study of the use and impact of performance measurement in Florida public libraries.* PhD diss., Florida State University. Quoted in J. Matthews 2004, 5.

Wiegand, Wayne A. 1986. *The politics of an emerging profession: The American Library Association, 1876–1917.* Contributions in Librarianship and Information Science, no. 56. New York: Greenwood. Quoted in McCook 2004, 49.

Wolfe, Alan. 1999. Bowling with others. Books. *New York Times* (October 17).

World Commission on Environment and Development. 1987. *Our common future.* Oxford Paperbacks. Oxford: Oxford University Press.

Zengerle, Jason. 1997. Investing in social capital. *Swarthmore College Bulletin Online* (September). www.swarthmore.edu/bulletin/archive/97/sept97/putnam.html.

ADDITIONAL RESOURCES

Adaptive Path: A UX Blog [blog]. www.adaptivepath.com/blog/.

Altschuld, James W., and Belle Ruth Witkin. 2000. *From needs assessment to action: Transforming needs into solution strategies.* Thousand Oaks, CA: Sage.

American Library Association. 1960. *The library-community project of the American Library Association.* Report, 1955–60. Chicago: American Library Association.

Anderson, Joe. 2005. Value propositions and libraries. March 21. http://webjunction.org/do/DisplayContent?id=1201.

Baker, Sharon L., and F. Wilfrid Lancaster. 1991. *The measurement and evaluation of library services.* Arlington, VA: Information Resources Press.

Balas, J. L. 2008. Social networks and the library community. *Computers in Libraries–Westport* 28 (4): 40–45.

Bell, Steven J. 2008a. Design thinking—A design approach to the delivery of outstanding service can help put the user experience first. *American Libraries* 39 (1): 44.

———. 2008b. Service design vs. experience design. *Designing Better Libraries* [blog]. August 29. http://dbl.lishost.org/blog/2008/08/29/service-design -vs-experience-design/.

Bell, Steven J., and John D. Shank. 2007. *Academic librarianship by design: A blended librarian's guide to the tools and techniques.* Chicago: American Library Association.

Blended Librarian [online community]. http://blendedlibrarian.org.

Borgmann, Albert. 1999. *Holding on to reality: The nature of information at the turn of the millennium.* Chicago: University of Chicago Press.

Brawner, Lee B., and Donald K. Beck Jr. 1996a. *Determining your public library's future size: A needs assessment and planning model.* Chicago: American Library Association.

———. 1996b. *If your last library building turned out like this, next time start with a needs assessment.* New York: American Library Trustee Association.

Buckland, Michael K. 1982. Concepts of library goodness. *Canadian Library Journal* 39 (April): 63–66.

Christensen, Karen, and David Levinson. 2003. *Encyclopedia of community: From the village to the virtual world.* Thousand Oaks, CA: Sage.

Diller, Stephen, Nathan Shedroff, and Darrel Rhea. 2006. *Making meaning: How successful businesses deliver meaningful customer experiences.* Berkeley, CA: New Riders.

Dresang, E. T., M. Gross, and L. E. Holt. 2003. Project CATE: Using outcome measures to assess school-age children's use of technology in urban public libraries; a collaborative research process. *Library and Information Science Research* 25 (1): 19–42.

Drucker, Peter F. 2001. *The essential Drucker: Selections from the management works of Peter F. Drucker.* New York: HarperBusiness.

Dudden, Rosalind F. 2007. *Using benchmarking, needs assessment, quality improvement, outcome measurement, and library standards: A how-to-do-it manual with CD-ROM.* New York: Neal-Schuman.

Garrett, Jesse James. 2003. *The elements of user experience: User-centered design for the Web.* Voices That Matter. New York: American Institute of Graphic Arts.

Gilchrist, Alison. 2004. *The well-connected community: A networking approach to community development.* Bristol: Policy Press.

Hernon, Peter, and Robert E. Dugan. 2002. *Outcomes assessment in your library.* Chicago: American Library Association.

Hildenbrand, S. 2000. Library feminism and library women's history: Activism and scholarship, equity and culture. *Libraries and Culture* 35:51–65.

Hill, Ann, and Julieta Dias Fisher. 2002. *Tooting your own horn: Web-based public relations for the 21st century librarian.* Worthington, OH: Linworth Publishing.

Hollywood, John S., and Kenneth N. McKay. 2003. *Managing information networks to meet user and mission needs.* Santa Monica, CA: RAND.

Holt, Glen E. 1999. *Public library partnerships: Mission-driven tools for 21st century success.* Gütersloh [Germany]: Bertelsmann Foundation.

Howard, Jeff. *Design for Service* [blog]. http://designforservice.wordpress

Jason, Leonard. 1997. *Community building: Values for a sustainable future.* Westport, CT: Praeger.

Johnson, Veronica A. 1986. *The public library and community needs ass.* Lansing: Library of Michigan.

Jones, Rebecca. 2000. Business plans: Roadmaps for growth and su. *Information Outlook* 4 (12): 22–20.

Kelley, Tom, and Jonathan Littman. 2001. *The art of innovation: I creativity from IDEO, America's leading design firm.* New Yor Books.

A Librarian at Every Table [online community]. http://shell.cas.usf
    .edu/~mccook/alaet/.
Librarians' Internet Index [website]. http://lii.org.
Library Success Wiki—Marketing [wiki]. www.libsuccess.org/index
    .php?title=Marketing.
Library 2.0 [online community]. http://library20.ning.com.
Liu, Lewis-Guodo. 2001. *The role and impact of the Internet on library and
    information services.* Contributions in Librarianship and Information
    Science, no. 96. Westport, CT: Greenwood.
Marshall, Chris E. 1978. *Needs assessment for social planning: Ideas and
    approaches.* Monticello, IL: Council of Planning Librarians.
Maxwell, Nancy Kalikow. 2006. *Sacred stacks: The higher purpose of libraries and
    librarianship.* Chicago: American Library Association.
McLean, M. 2007. Library 2.0 and libraries building community initiatives in
    Australia. *Computers in Libraries—Annual Conference and Exhibition USA*
    (Conf 22): 28–35.
McLean, Neil, and Clare Wilde. 2001. Evaluating library performance: The
    search for relevance. *Australian Academic and Research Libraries* 22 (3): 201.
McLean, Scott L., David A. Schultz, and Manfred B. Steger. 2002. *Social capital:
    Critical perspectives on community and "Bowling Alone."* New York: New York
    University Press.
Monroe, Margaret Ellen, and Gail A. Schlachter. 1982. *The service imperative
    for libraries: Essays in honor of Margaret E. Monroe.* Littleton, CO: Libraries
    Unlimited.
Neuber, Keith A. 1980. *Needs assessment: A model for community planning.* Sage
    Human Services Guides, v. 14. Beverly Hills, CA: Sage.
———. 1985. *Needs assessment: A model for community planning.* Beverly Hills,
    CA: University of Michigan School of Social Work / Sage.
Nicholas, David. 2000. *Assessing information needs: Tools, techniques, and concepts
    for the Internet age.* London: Aslib Information Management.
Oldenburg, Ray. 2001. *Celebrating the third place: Inspiring stories about the "great
    good places" at the heart of our communities.* New York: Marlowe.
Outsell, Inc. 2002. *ToolKit: The why and how of needs assessment.* Information
    about Information Briefing, v. 5, no. 16. Burlingame, CA: Outsell, Inc.
Petruzzelli, Barbara Whitney. 2005. *Real-life marketing and promotion strategies
    in college libraries: Connecting with campus and community.* Binghamton, NY:
    Haworth Information Press.
Pew Internet and American Life Project. 2007. Internet adoption (a chart
    showing the U.S. Internet penetration over time). www.pewInternet.org/
    trends/Internet_Adoption_4.26.07.pdf.

Pine, B. Joseph, and James H. Gilmore. 1999. *The experience economy: Work is theatre and every business a stage.* Boston: Harvard Business School Press.

Pink, Daniel H. 2005. *A whole new mind: Moving from the information age to the conceptual age.* New York: Riverhead Books.

Portugal, Franklin H. 2000. *Valuating information intangibles: Measuring the bottom line contribution of librarians and information professionals.* Washington, DC: Special Libraries Association.

Pungitore, Verna Leah. 1995. *Innovation and the library: The adoption of new ideas in public libraries.* Contributions in Librarianship and Information Science, no. 86. Westport, CT: Greenwood.

Putnam, Robert D. 1993. The prosperous community: Social capital and public life. *American Prospect* 13:35–42.

Putnam, Robert D., Lewis M. Feldstein, and Don Cohen. 2003. *Better together: Restoring the American community.* New York: Simon and Schuster.

Reed, Sally Gardner. 2005. FOLUSA: The advocacy campaign (March 21). http://webjunction.org/do/DisplayContent?id=8591.

Rheingold, Howard. 1993. *The virtual community: Homesteading on the electronic frontier.* Reading, MA: Addison-Wesley.

Rippel, Chris. 2004. What libraries can learn from bookstores (June 24). http://webjunction.org/do/DisplayContent?id=1191.

Rubin, Rhea Joyce. 2006. *Demonstrating results: Using outcome measurement in your library.* PLA Results Series. Chicago: American Library Association.

Saskatchewan. 1993. *Needs assessment of the library's community: A bibliography.* Regina: Provincial Library, Saskatchewan Municipal Government.

Smith, Marc A., and Peter Kollock. 1999. *Communities in cyberspace.* London: Routledge.

St. Paul Community Literacy Consortium. 2004. *Community needs assessment: Library services for underserved communities.* [St. Paul, MN]: St. Paul Community Literacy Consortium.

State Library of Victoria, Library Board of Victoria, and Victorian Public Library Network. 2005. *Libraries building communities: The vital contribution of Victoria's public libraries; a research report for the Library Board of Victoria and the Victorian Public Library Network.* [Melbourne]: State Library of Victoria.

Stern, Gary J. 1990. *Marketing workbook for nonprofit organizations.* St. Paul, MN: Amherst H. Wilder Foundation.

Thorsen, Jeanne. 1998. Community studies: Raising the roof and other recommendations. *Acquisitions Librarian* 10 (20): 5.

United States. President's Research Committee on Social Trends. 1933. *Recent social trends in the United States; report of the President's Research Committee on Social Trends.* New York: McGraw-Hill.

Walker, Chris, and Carlos A. Manjarrez. 2003. *Partnerships for free choice learning: Public libraries, museums, and public broadcasters working together.* Washington, DC: The Urban Institute; Evanston, IL: Urban Libraries Council. www.urban.org/UploadedPDF/410661_partnerships_for_free _choice_learning.pdf.

Walters, Suzanne. 2004. *Library marketing that works.* New York: Neal-Schuman.

WebJunction [online community]. www.webjunction.org.

Weinreich, Nedra Kline. 1999. *Hands-on social marketing: A step-by-step guide.* Thousand Oaks, CA: Sage.

Woodward, Jeannette A. 2005. *Creating the customer-driven library: Building on the bookstore model.* Chicago: American Library Association.

World Bank. 2002. What is social capital? [website]. www1.worldbank.org/ prem/poverty/scapital/whatsc.htm.

Young, Kimball L. 2002. *21st century library needs assessment: Final report.* Salt Lake City: Utah State Library Division. http://library.utah .gov/21stcentury.html.

INDEX

You may also be interested in

Small Business and the Public Library: An essential resource in difficult economic times, this book targets libraries endeavoring to assist users entering or already involved in the small business community. Whether patrons need resources to start their own business, search for a new job, or locate demographic statistics to help them market their existing product, this resource will help you answer their questions and meet their needs.

Creating Your Library Brand: In the new media mix, libraries need to stand up and effectively communicate their benefits as a preferred provider of information and entertainment resources. By following the step-by-step guidance of Elisabeth Doucett, branding pro turned librarian, you can begin to develop branding that makes a difference. Tips, suggestions for success, and answers to frequently asked questions ensure your team collaborates on a library brand that will bring more patrons through the door!

Marketing Today's Academic Library: The guiding principle of this book is that marketing should focus on the lifestyle of the user, showcasing how the library fits into the daily life of the student. Written in a concise and engaging manner that speaks to popular anxiety points about new marketing techniques, this book is filled with tips and strategies that academic librarians can use to communicate with students, surpassing students' expectations of their library experience.

Creating the Customer-Driven Academic Library: Jeannette Woodward's strategies center on keeping the customer's point of view in focus at all times to help you integrate technology to meet the needs of today's students and faculty, reevaluate the role and function of library service desks, implement staffing strategies to match customer expectations, and create new and effective promotional materials. As you are faced with marketing to a generation of students who log on rather than walk in, this cutting-edge book supplies the tools needed to keep customers coming through the door.

Check out these and other great titles at www.alastore.ala.org!